Dedication

I dedicate this book to my late mom and dad, Paulina and Boniface Okafor, my late uncles Festus Ogbonna Okafor, Chief Gregory Uchendu Maduka, and Ichie Michael Nkemakolam Maduka – aka "Be kind." They sowed the seed of God's love and compassion in my heart. They were loving, kind, and generous. Their witness of faith and friendly attitude towards everyone impacted me so positively that I wanted to be like them right from my childhood.

Also, I dedicate this book to all my friends, the benefactors of Boniface and Paulina Okafor Memorial Hospital & Family Care Program (BAPOM Hospital), and to all people of goodwill who generously give of themselves to make the lives of others better and to make our world a better place to live for all.

Finally, I dedicate this book to prisoners and anyone who is broken or struggling. May they find healing, hope, and strength in Jesus Christ, who came that we may have life and have it more abundantly.

WE ARE CHOSEN

God's Plan for His People

Interpreting life experiences from

God's perspective

By

FR. TOOCHUKWU BARTHOLOMEW OKAFOR

Paulette Scheme, Editing and Layout

We Are Chosen

Nihil Obstat: + Brian Joseph Dunn
Archbishop of Halifax-Yarmouth
July 2022

Cover design: Tamara Marie Freeman
Cover photo: Frank Scheme
Back cover photo: Ana Luisa de Arruda Darcie

tellwell

Tellwell Talent
www.tellwell.ca

ISBN
978-0-2288-8341-8 (Hardcover)
978-0-2288-8407-1 (Paperback)
978-0-2288-8408-8 (eBook)

Contents

Acknowledgements

I praise and thank God for the gift of my life and for my vocation to the priesthood. I sincerely thank Archbishops Anthony Mancini, Terry Prendergast and Brian Dunn who made it possible for me to come and work as a missionary in the Archdiocese of Halifax-Yarmouth. I appreciate your love and support in my priestly ministry.

There is a song in Spanish that says, "Yo quiero tener un million de amigos, asi mas fuerte podre cantar." (I want to have a million friends so that I can sing louder.) Well, I may not have a million friends, but I can say that I have been blessed and privileged to have a few good friends. These, for me, are worth more than a million friends; they help me to sing louder. I sincerely express my heartfelt gratitude to all my friends. It will be impossible to mention all of them here, so, I can only mention a few – Fr. Marcellinus Onyejekwe, CMF, Fr. Chinedu Chukwu, Josie Ritcey, Fr. Matthew Ihuoma, Fr. Anthony Okolo, CMF, Fr. John Ezenwankwor, CMF, Fr. Bruno Onyekuru, CMF, Fr. Wence Madu, CMF, Fr. Anthony Azinta, CMF, Fr. Jude Anyaehie, CMF, Fr. Henry Omonisaye, CMF, Fr. Jude Arinze, CMF, Fr. Venatius Umennebuaku, CMF, Fr. George Ekwuru, CMF, Fr. Henry Ebo, CMF, Fr. Mike Eke, CMF, Fr. Nicholas Chinweze, CMF, Serge & Shelly De-Serres, Sr. Genevieve Nwaizu, Sr. Joannes Uzoma, Dr. Alcira Alba Acevedo & Fred Panasik, Edilma Polanco, Elaine & David Young, Jim & Anne McLevey, Lorraine

Coulombe, Rosemary & Gary Moore, John McMichael, RoseAnn Hetherington, Gail Tims & Ralph Coppola, Elizabeth Morrisey, Lucile Bourque-Lampier, Heather Pettipas, Marguerite & Hubert Fougere, Marie Mattie, Pat Proctor, Debbie & Steve Daigle, Dana & Elena Sponogle, Dr. Ejike Mgbenkemdi, Prof. Oby Omeje, Dr. Adaobi Eze, Prof. Chidi Oguamanam, Bartholomew Azubike, Isabel Ortiz & Enrique Nieves De Moya, Nydia Ariza & Ivan Marquez, Nora Montoya, Nuria, Sarita, Angelica Vianna, Angela Maria Palechor Morales, Yesim Barrios, Angie Barandica, Sulima Rojas, Fr. Vincent Amusuo, Fr. Charles Offor, Fr. Vincent Onyekelu, Chiemerie Victor Alum, Nora & Cyril Muise, Audrey & Mike Myrick, Fr. Paul Morris, Fr. James Mallon, Ron Huntley, Patricia Cosgrove, Ron & Dora Gallant, Wayne O'Leary, Fr. Patrick Salah, Deacon Bernie Coffin, Deacon Larry & Linda Worthen, Bill & Mary Anne Grady, Amy Graves, Dr. Naan Ferguson, Laura & Peter Butler, Fr. Paul Nwaeze, Sydney Mifflin, George & Duana Mbamalu, Christie Duru, Fr. Jude Kabiri, Paulette & Frank Scheme, Mary & Jim Colford, parishioners of Christ the King Parish, Dartmouth, NS, Benefactors of BAPOM Hospital and Family Care Program, parishioners of John of the Cross Parish, Eastern shore, parishioners of Our Lady of Chiquiquira Barranquilla Colombia, parishioners of Our Lady of Mount Carmel Espiriella Tumaco, parishioners of Jesus Nazareno Medellin, Catholic Women's League (CWL), Knights of Columbus (KoC), African Mass Community, Archdiocese of Halifax-Yarmouth and the Claretian Missionaries, etc.

I sincerely thank my siblings/family – Honorable Sheriff & Ogechi Okafor, Chimamaka Juliana & Ugochukwu Diribe, Bernadeth Chika & Sunday Eresi Shedrack, Edwin & Favour Okafor, my nephews and nieces, uncle Theophilus Egbeocha Obi and all my relatives. Also, I want to thank all those who contributed to making this dream a reality, especially Eucharia Remy who read my manuscript and made valuable suggestions. I see each of you as a God-sent gift in my life. And permit me to say that, if you have ever wondered what your mission in life is, your coming into my life and all the help and support you've given and continue to give to me is one of the reasons God brought you into this world. Thank you for saying yes to him as our Blessed Mother Mary did. Thank you for your kindness, generosity, and unconditional love. My life and ministry are prosperous and happier because you're part of it. Thank you for accepting me with my strengths and weaknesses and being patient with me. It gives me great freedom and joy to know that you and I are chosen, loved, and blessed by God, as he has shown me through each one of you - my family members, friends, and parishioners. For this, I am eternally grateful.

Foreword

On Fr. Toochukwu's 25th anniversary of priestly ordination, I am pleased to offer him my congratulations. For more than half of these years, Fr. Toochukwu has exercised his pastoral care for God's people in the Archdiocese of Halifax-Yarmouth, where I, as the archbishop at the time, accepted his offer to serve in our local Church. I thank him for his continued commitment and dedication. His presence in our midst has been faithful, fruitful, and blessed.

As Fr. Toochukwu reflects on his years of ministry, he has chosen to share his thoughts with his friends and family in this personal re-reading of his life's journey. Through a series of chapters, which read like vignettes of his life, Fr. Toochukwu sees, recognizes, and gives testimony to the providence of God working in the various circumstances and experiences which marked his journey. He highlights God's guiding presence through the significant people who shaped and dedicated his early life and his first educational efforts. Perhaps what stands out most is the powerful influence of Fr. Toochukwu's family and particularly the impact of his mother.

Fr. Toochukwu does not avoid sharing his failures and early disappointments, including his turning away from religious practice and rejection of the Church and clergy. What is striking in this account is to see Fr. Toochukwu's heart change as he was touched early by the hand of God. In hindsight, Fr. Toochukwu sees the mysterious action of the Holy Spirit working in all circumstances, including his setbacks and mainly how grace flowed back into his life through the words and example of many people, not always the pious, but always God's instruments.

I was personally moved by Fr. Toochukwu's openness and freedom to share his story. Perhaps this is because he speaks from the heart as a man, a priest, and a pastor. Fr. Toochukwu reveals his faith and spiritual experiences that have clearly left their mark on how he ministers to others. It is evident from the style of this book that the Catholic Charismatic Renewal movement played a significant role in the way his faith is lived, how God is understood, and the life of the Church appreciated. Whether or not one is drawn to this way of expression and Christian life, we cannot miss the fact that for Fr. Toochukwu, his whole life and ministry reflect the Holy Spirit alive and active in his pastoral care of those whom he serves. In sharing his thoughts, Fr. Toochukwu testifies to many values but, above all, to the centrality of joy and trust in his life.

When I welcomed Fr. Toochukwu into our Archdiocese, I welcomed a priest willing to be a missionary in our local Church. In our time of collaboration, I came to appreciate his dedication and fidelity. In this book of reflection on twenty-five years of priestly life, Fr. Toochukwu has opened his heart to all with, I hope, beneficial effect.

A characteristic of Fr. Toochukwu's personality is his smile and the joy he brings with his well-known greeting, "Are you happy?" His happiness is infectious, and it brings great encouragement. This local church has been blessed by Fr. Toochukwu's priestly ministry. May he continue his service for many years to come.

+Anthony Mancini
Archbishop Emeritus of Halifax-Yarmouth

Father Toochukwu Okafor

25th Anniversary of Priestly Ordination

Images captured from livestream masses at St. Thomas More Church, Dartmouth, N.S.

Thoughts about "We Are Chosen"

I am grateful for the opportunity of writing a few thoughts about the book *"We are Chosen – Interpreting life experiences from God's Perspective"* – a reflection on the life of Fr. Toochukwu Okafor, a priest of the Archdiocese of Halifax-Yarmouth.

An autobiography is one type of biography that tells its author's life story. It fits a genre of spiritual reflections on one's life to discover God's presence and hand. While autobiographical works can take many forms, from the intimate writing made during life that was not necessarily intended for publication (including letters, diaries, journals, memoirs, and reminiscences) to a formal book-length autobiography, this work provides a combination of intimate memoirs and reflections upon a life lived in the presence of God.

While the most common purpose of a brief autobiography is to depict a vital challenge or event in the author's life, Fr. Toochukwu wants to highlight how God has worked in his life and how one can see every experience in their life as a steppingstone for success. From his birth and early childhood, Fr. Toochukwu provides a variety of stories to "recall the goodness and mercy of God in my life and ministry and give thanks for all the beautiful things he has done in me and through me (p.22).

It is often said that an autobiography is not the story of a life but the recreation or the discovery of one. In writing of his life's experience, Fr. Toochukwu has provided a journal of discovery of himself as loved by God and as one who the Lord has accompanied throughout the experience of his life.

In some way, this book is a collection of well-rehearsed anecdotes. But more importantly, it provides the writer's conception of life as he has lived it in Nigeria, Colombia, and Nova Scotia. The personal stories shared are forged into a graceful, coherent narrative that conveys the larger story of his life.

These stories function as snapshots or windows into the heart of a person. They portray a person of faith who wants to proclaim how God has worked in his life. These stories reveal a person who has struggled to discover the will of God in his life. They show a person who is convinced of certain truths connected to his faith.

I take this opportunity to congratulate Fr. Toochukwu on the 25th anniversary of his ordination to the priesthood. This book is a beautiful tribute to God's blessings on Fr. Toochukwu during these twenty-five years. May those who read these stories be stirred to seek how God is present in their own lives. May each reader discover how God calls each of us to know the consequences of living our faith and to treasure the importance of reflecting on the experiences and issues that touch our lives daily.

+ Brian Joseph Dunn

Archbishop of Halifax-Yarmouth

Thoughts about "We Are Chosen"

"Holy Communion" is not just what we Catholics receive in the Eucharist. Holy Communion is the daily aim of every Christian as we seek to live a life of purpose, meaning, and joy. Life is a struggle at times. Life apart from God is also a struggle, and worse, it lacks purpose and meaning beyond our death. We cannot live in communion with God if we are not aware of our identity. "We are Chosen" is the perfect title for Fr. Toochukwu's book and the witness within these pages. It is good news to know that you and I are Chosen and that we can see God's hand at work in all our life experiences – good and bad alike!

I have worked with Fr. Toochukwu and his team at Christ the King Parish in Nova Scotia for the last few years as their parish leadership coach and then intimately as a part of Fr. Toochukwu's leadership team. I got to experience firsthand the abounding joy that Fr. Toochukwu lives every day, and I mean every day! Joy is a life strategy Fr. Toochukwu uses to deal with suffering, difficulty, setbacks, and uncertainty. It is not that Fr. Toochukwu does not get knocked down. He knows who to turn to for the strength to get back up and keep going. Being a parish priest or any leader in the church these days is not for the faint at heart.

Fr. Toochukwu's story of faith mirrors the story of so many of the faithful who are willing to self-reflect, be vulnerably honest with themselves, and who, against all odds, persevere. Becoming the person we know we are called to be is often messy. The way to freedom is the road of truth when we face our reality and surrender everything to Jesus; look out because miracles abound!

As missionary disciples filled with the Holy Spirit, we have access to the POWER of God, and God often calls us to do things that we cannot do without him. This life of faith calls us to be naturally supernatural.

So many members of the clergy and lay faithful have lost their zeal and forgotten their true identity to the church's detriment.

Until you and I dare to live the grace given to us by God, our impact on the world around us will remain insignificant. God is begging us to trust him, receive the forgiveness he offers, put the past behind us and live together in the power of the Holy Spirit.

This book is a miraculous testimony of how God works to redeem us, sets us right with him and others, and places a call on our life that is truly exhilarating. The stories in this book will cause you to reflect on who you are when everything else is stripped away and to realize that you are loved; your life has a purpose because you are Chosen.

Ron Huntley
Co-author of *Unlocking Your Parish*
www.ronhuntley.com

Introduction

Parents and grandparents are often worried when their children or grandchildren stop practicing their faith or choose a wrong path that might endanger their lives, separate them from God, and ruin their future careers. Some young people and adults sometimes face life challenges and crises that impact their lives negatively, leaving them disoriented, broken, empty, and sad. Such individuals often seek how to make meaning out of life. They grapple with fundamental questions like, "Why am I here on earth? What is the purpose of my life?" Perhaps you are among those asking these soul-searching questions, or you know someone doing so. You have had many experiences in your life, some of which are positive and exciting though some may have been very painful and difficult. You may be wondering, "why did this happen to me, why did God allow bad things to happen to me," or "why do bad things happen to innocent people," etc.? Well, I don't pretend to have answers to these questions. However, I wish to say to you, "There must be a reason behind it, so do not give up hope." I wish to suggest that you look at those events and circumstances not just from your perspective but from the perspective of God. When looked at with the lens of faith, you discover that there is a reason why God allowed each of your experiences to happen in the way they did and at the time they took place. This is not suggesting determinism or negating our free will; it rather indicates that the way you choose to see and respond to those experiences can either make you or break you. Sharing some of my experiences, family background, and struggles may help you see where I am coming from.

Each time I attend a gathering or share my experiences with other people, one of the common questions I get is, "Why did you become a priest, and when did you feel the calling to become a priest?" Each time, after sharing my vocation story and experiences in the ministry, the next question I hear is, "Have you written a book?" "No," I would reply, and then the next question, "Why have you not written a book?" One day, some family friends from St. Thomas More Church in Dartmouth, Nova Scotia – Rosemary and Gary Moore, Steward and Elaine LaRusic invited me for dinner; as always, they asked about my vocation journey, my family background, and why I chose to become a priest. After sharing my story with them, Stewart said, "Father, you should write a book." He even suggested a title, and we laughed over it. Afterward, each time he saw me at Mass, he asked me, "Have you started?" He even promised to buy the first copy.

I must say it was his constant encouragement and my passion to give hope to parents and grandparents who are worried about their children who have strayed in their faith, as well as giving hope to young people who are struggling or have made wrong choices in life that gave birth to this book. As I celebrate the twenty-fifth anniversary of my priestly ordination, I feel it is an opportunity to reflect on my life and vocation journey. It is also an opportunity to recall the goodness and mercy of God in my life and ministry and give thanks for all the beautiful things he has done in me and through me. In Psalm 107:1, the Psalmist says, "Oh give thanks to the Lord for he is good; for his great love endures forever!" I have truly experienced the unconditional love of God in many ways through my family, friends, and parishioners in every place I have ministered. The support and encouragement I received and continue to receive have been phenomenal. I believe God answered the prayers my dad and mom said for me before they died. Both gave me a special blessing before they passed away. I wish all parents would do the same - pray with and for their children all the time and bestow on them their blessings before they die. Such prayers and blessings are powerful and are never forgotten.

I thank God for my family and each of my friends who motivated me to write my life experiences. I learned from them the power of encouragement. As you read the following pages, I encourage you to reflect on your own story – the purpose and mission of your life. Think about the individuals who have been sources of encouragement in your life. Give thanks to God for them and, if possible, call them to express your gratitude. Also, think of the people you would like to encourage in your life. Help them develop their potential to the fullest capacity that God had in mind when he sent them into this world. You may never understand the positive impact your words of encouragement can have on the individual; it is effective and changes lives. Testimonies abound about people whose lives have been transformed because someone encouraged them. And one thing fascinating to note is that practicing the art of encouragement changes not only the other person but also your life and brings you joy.

As I look back on the story of my life, it is clear to me that neither I nor the circumstances of my life are a product of chance. The first chapter, "You are not an accident," reminds us that God planned everything about us even before we were conceived. Chapter two focuses on my call to the priesthood, which started in my early childhood. Chapter three reveals that God works in mysterious ways. His ways are not our ways. Thus, we can find him in places and people where we least expect him; this I discovered through my contact with a prisoner. That experience is narrated in chapter four, when detention led to conversion. Chapter five is about a voice I heard that I interpret as God's voice because that voice brought me closer to him. Chapter six discusses how God can make a way where there seems no way, for nothing is impossible for God. If God has a specific mission for you, one way or another, he will align circumstances in your life that will enable you to accomplish it, even when all odds seem to be against it.

Chapter seven is about some miracles of healing I experienced in my ministry, which remind us that miracles do happen, and that Jesus is faithful to his promises. He said, "In my name, you shall lay your hands on the sick, and they will be healed" (Mk. 16:17-18). Chapter eight is focused on love - the universal language. Everyone understands love - no matter their colour, culture, gender or religion. I came to the full realization of this fundamental truth when I went on a mission to Colombia. I couldn't understand Spanish, yet I was able to connect and communicate with the people through the language of love. The same language of love makes it possible for me to connect with people everywhere I go. As long as you have a love of God in your heart and you are willing to share it, you will connect with many people.

Chapter nine is about my mission to Canada, which has been a source of many blessings to me, my people, and the people I serve, as seen in the testimony of healing as a Christmas gift and other testimonies. Chapter ten narrates how some people's missions are accomplished at death, perhaps without their family's knowledge. Chapter eleven shows how God meets our needs, which confirms the Psalmist in Psalm 23:1: "The Lord is my shepherd, there is nothing I shall want."

Chapter twelve reflects on the importance of remaining connected with the Lord and offers some of the spiritual exercises that help me stay connected. Chapter thirteen affirms that you are of great value to God. He loves you; therefore, you should always be happy. Such perspectives about life help keep you focused on Jesus Christ, knowing that you have been chosen and blessed by God. It also gives peace of mind and hope for a better future. No matter what happens in your life, if you look at it from faith in Jesus Christ, who is the Alpha and Omega, the beginning and the end, you will see Him at work in every circumstance and experience. This confirms the saying, "Those who put everything in God's hand will eventually see God's hand in everything."

Chapter fourteen discusses the birth of the Boniface and Paulina Okafor Memorial Hospital and Family Care Program, which has the primary objective of providing subsidized healthcare and support to poor and needy families in Nigeria, particularly in my hometown Isuochi. The appendix describes this in further detail.

My aim in writing this book is primarily to thank God and encourage you never to lose hope, knowing that God has a plan for your life, a plan of peace and a future filled with hope (Jer. 29:11). If you trust Jesus and tightly hold on to him, he will never let you down; he will save you and give you abundant life and joy. And you will discover that each of the experiences in your life can be an opportunity for growth and a steppingstone for success, and it can help you make other people's lives better.

As you read, consider these questions:

1. Do you know you are *Chosen by God* and that he has a plan for your life?
2. What is the purpose of your life or your mission?
3. Who and what are you living for?
4. As to your relationship with God, do you see him as a friend or an exigent master?
5. Do you spend some time each day with God in prayer and listening to his Word in the scriptures?

6. How do you interpret the events and experiences of your life - do you see God's hand in them, or do you think they are a coincidence?
7. What is your attitude when things don't go your way or as planned?
8. Are you satisfied with your life, or are you still searching?
9. To whom do you go when life is messy? Have you tried Jesus Christ and our Blessed Mother Mary?
10. Do you find joy in helping people, and are you grateful for your blessings?

If this book can help you, the reader, in any way to see God's hand at work in the different life experiences at every stage of your life and consequently be encouraged to grow in friendship with Jesus and live a fulfilled life, it will have achieved its goal. Please give me feedback or send me your testimony if reading this book impacts your life positively. Your testimony could be a source of encouragement and hope for others. If you would like me to share my testimony with your prayer group, parish community, young people/adults at school or in prison, AA group, etc., please contact me at:

wearechosen2022@yahoo.com

1

You are not an accident

"Now the word of the Lord came to me saying, "Before I formed you in the womb I knew you, and before you were born, I consecrated you; I appointed you a prophet to the nations" (Jer.1:4-5 - NRSVB).

This passage perfectly confirms that your coming into being is not a mistake. God, the Master Planner, designed you and he had a plan and a mission for you even before you were conceived or born, just as he has for every other person he created. No one is here by chance, and nothing happens by accident. You did not choose your place of birth, parents, siblings, relatives, etc. God chose them for you for a specific purpose. As life unfolds and with every day and year that passes, you understand more and more why God brought you into being and why he put you in your family. Reading a bit about my life story may help you see the truth behind this claim and perhaps help you reflect on your own life to see how God's hand has been at work through different experiences in your life and your family.

I was born in Umudim Ngodo-Isuochi, Ummunneochi LGA, Abia State, Nigeria. My community belongs to one of the major tribes in Nigeria known as the "*Igbos*." Nigeria has more than 250 ethnic groups, each with its language, socio-cultural, traditional and religious beliefs. Though these diversities are valuable and enriching, sometimes they make unity and peaceful coexistence very difficult because of some fundamentalists' pseudo-beliefs and ideologies. My tribal language or mother tongue is also known as *Igbo*. Each tribe attaches great importance to its language and cultural heritage and could not easily communicate with other tribes until the advent of British colonial masters, who introduced English as our national language. However, only those who have a formal education can speak English. Another version of the language is called Pidgin English, an adulteration or mixture of some English words with other tribal languages like *Igbo, Hausa, or Yoruba.*

In *Igbo* philosophy and cultural anthropology, language and name play a vital role in understanding the identity and characteristics of a person, family, and community. Through names, the Igbo people express and communicate their feelings, desires and knowledge among themselves and other supernatural beings – like God or the ancestral spirits. Thus, the name(s) given to someone at birth most often reflects the circumstances surrounding the person's birth, the desires of the parents, or the person's mission. Sometimes, a person's name is prophetic because there could be a fulfillment of the expressed desires and aspirations in the individual's life. That is reflected in my name, as will be seen later.

Just like the importance of a name, Igbo cultural anthropology sees life as *ihe omimi,* literally meaning a mystery. Hence 'life' is considered sacred, and great value is attached to it. The human being is regarded as the highest expression of this '*ihe omimi*' or '*life'* and should be treated like a treasure greater than material things. My great-grandfather's name, '*MADUKAKU'*, which means "Man is greater than wealth," expresses this belief. Therefore, our people would insist that human beings should be given more importance than material things.

My parents had eight children, of which I am the fifth child, although now I am the youngest after the death of my three younger siblings. Below is a picture of us from left to the right: Toochukwu, Bernadeth, Sheriff Sylva, Chimamaka Juliana, and Edwin.

We have a very close relationship in our family. Our culture and family values are collectivist; thus, we try to care for each other and support one another following the Igbo philosophy of "*Umunna bu ike,*" meaning, "*Brotherhood is strength,*" and "*Onye aghana nwanne ya,*" which means *"Do not leave your brother or sister behind."* This worldview on solidarity is a necessity since many people are poor and have no government socio-economic assistance to help them take care of their essential needs. This was the dominant culture of my people when I was born in 1967. During that time, my tribe, *Igbos*, known as "Biafra," wanted to secede from the rest of the country, Nigeria, because they felt they were socio-politically and economically marginalized. This led to the Nigerian – Biafran war. Lt. Col. Emeka Odumegwu Ojukwu, a military officer from the *Igbo* tribe, led *Biafra* in a war that lasted for three years. Millions of people died during the war, not just because of the bombings and shootings, but due to starvation and malnutrition because Nigeria blocked all the sources of international aid to the *Igbos*. Most of those who died were children and nursing mothers.

My community (the whole village) was displaced, and my parents ran into the woods searching for safety, leaving behind all their belongings. At the time of my birth, there was no access to hospitals or clinics; there was no medical care or even necessities of life. Everybody was living in fear, and my parents couldn't go anywhere to search for food. Unfortunately, due to a lack of proper care and hygiene, my mum got an infection that forced her to stop breastfeeding me. I was told that I cried a lot at that time, especially at night. That constituted a great danger for the whole family since the Nigerian army might hear the cry and come after us. They would use some clothes to cover my mouth to stop me from crying, which was emotionally traumatizing and unhealthy for a child. It was a horrible experience for us, and everybody thought we would die. Providentially, we survived the war, and my parents gave thanks to God for saving our lives. This was reflected in the name they gave me – "*Toochukwu*" – which means *"Praise God."*

One remarkable thing about my birth is that, before I was born, my dad was not a Christian, but after my birth and our survival from the war, he decided to convert to Christianity. He became actively engaged in our parish as one of the sacristans, ushers, and parish leaders. God works in mysterious ways. Even though the war was evil, horrific, and devastating, God used it to touch my dad's heart and drew him into a relationship with Jesus Christ. It is said that God can write on a crooked line; in other words, he can make good out of the evil things that happen in our lives. So, if you are going through tough times or situations that seem insurmountable, do not despair, for the God of the mountain is also the God in the valley.

Rebuilding after the war was very hard as many families lost all they owned. Most people were left with nothing; they could only rely on the aid from the Irish missionary priests at the time. My parents were mainly farmers and, after each harvest, my dad would distribute yams to all the poor people and widows in our village and my mom would prepare some food and ask me to take it to the beggars at our market square. Our house was a home for all, and even though my mom had no formal education, she memorized almost all of the Catechism of the Catholic Church and the Bible. She had a great love for the Word of God, a virtue she learned from my grandmother, Esther Obi. My grandmother was a very devout woman who made the Bible her daily companion. As a boy, I often saw her reading the Bible, and I wondered why she was so 'addicted' to that big book. The Bible looked so big to me then. Now, I realize that my grandma was drawing her spiritual strength and courage to face the struggles and challenges of the day from the Bible.

In those days, Catholics didn't read the Bible very often, but because my mom had been a Methodist before converting to Catholicism, she was brought up with my grandma's culture of studying the Word of God in Sunday school. Eventually, my mom became one of the Sunday school teachers in our village church. I learned from my mom that, though formal education is essential, those who didn't have that opportunity could still develop their potential and use their natural gifts and talents to love and serve God and humanity. My mom prepared and sponsored many children for Baptism and Confirmation. She would invite all her godchildren for a meal every year during Easter and Christmas. Sometimes there were about twenty children or more who attended the party. As a child, I looked forward to that party because it was an opportunity to get some treats like pop, candies, and biscuits that we usually would not have in our family.

Mom and dad helped the priest aid the poor and needy of our local church and community. I admired the social outreach and spiritual services both the priest and my parents were rendering to the poor people, and I wanted to become like them. Little did they know that they were sowing the seed of a priestly vocation in my heart through their actions and life of witnessing. Indeed, actions speak louder than words. Parents, grandparents, and guardians can significantly impact their children's lives when they serve in their communities and introduce their children to a life of faith and service by getting them involved. No wonder the book of Proverb says, "Teach a child the way he should go, and he will not stray from it even when he is old" (Proverbs 22:6 - NCB). My mom and dad could have easily delivered those necessities to the recipients, but they chose to involve my siblings and me. It was their way of letting us see that many are less privileged and suffering more than ourselves. I guess they wanted us to learn from an early age the value of solidarity and generosity with the less privileged.

That reminds me of what Jesus did when he performed the miracle of the multiplication of the loaves and fish and fed the multitude as narrated in Mathew 14:13-21. After Jesus had given thanks for the five loaves and two fishes, he said prayers and gave them to his disciples to distribute to the crowd. He could have done it himself, but he engaged his disciples to show that he needed human instruments to provide for the poor and needy. Each time I visited those people, I greatly appreciated what we had. The experience also taught me that we have a moral and social obligation to care for the poor and to help them in their need. Even though they didn't tell us why they involved us in distributing the items, I believe my parents wanted us to learn to be content with what we had, no matter how little that was. They always told my siblings and me not to complain when they didn't meet all our needs, but that we should instead be thankful, as gratitude is the key to happy living.

My dad and mom taught us that we should not be indifferent to the plight of the poor in our midst, and even though we didn't have much, we could share the little we had. It always made a deep impression on me when I saw the joy of those people as they received the gifts. They thanked God and prayed that God bless my parents and their children. I owe most of the blessings and favours I receive from people today to my parents' generosity and kindness to others. I can assure you without equivocation that your acts of kindness to those in need will never be forgotten; you will be rewarded in your children and grandchildren here in this world and in the world to come. As Proverbs says, "Whoever gives to the poor will lack nothing but one who turns a blind eye will get many a curse" (Proverbs 28:27 – NRSVB).

My parents taught us that when we give, it should be a sacrifice made in love and with joy. Such an act of giving makes us become like God, who sacrificed His only Son for the world's salvation. St. John put it succinctly when he said, "For God so loved the world that he gave his only Son, so that everyone who believes in him may not perish but may have eternal life" (John 3:16 - NRSVB). Although my parents had no money, they had a great love for God and their neighbours and, like Jesus, they taught us that those are the two great commandments. They would always remind us of eternal life with these words: "No matter what you do in life, never forget that this world is not your home. You are destined for eternal life with Jesus, so focus on him and do not let anyone or anything deprive you of heaven."

Suggested action: Reflect on your family dynamics – is there love, peace and unity in your family? Is there any area of your life or family life where you need Jesus to bring his healing mercy? You may take a moment to write them down and present them to God in prayer.

Prayer: Dear God, thank you for the gift of my life and family and all the families worldwide. Please bless all families with your love, peace and unity. Bring your healing mercy where it is needed most and help us to know that we are chosen. Give us the grace to achieve the purpose for which you brought us into this world and into our respective families. Amen!

2

Call to the priesthood

"We know that all things work together for good for those who love God, who are called according to his purpose. For those he foreknew he also predestined to be conformed to the image of his Son, in order that he might be the firstborn within a large family… What then are we to say about these things? If God is for us, who is against us? … Who will bring any charge against God's elect? … Who is to condemn? … Who will separate us from the love of Christ? … For I am convinced that neither death, nor life, nor angels, nor rulers, nor things present, nor things to come, nor powers, nor height, nor depth, nor anything else in all creation will be able to separate us from the love of God in Christ Jesus our Lord" (Romans 8:28-38 - NRSVB).

This is another scripture passage that I cherish very much. When I reflect on my life from childhood to the present, I see God's hand even in the seemingly negative and painful experiences I struggled through. Therefore, I can say with St. Paul that "We know that all things work together for good for those who love God" (Romans 8:28 - NRSVB), and the past events of my life support this point. When I finished primary school at the age of twelve, I decided to enter the minor seminary to undergo formation to the priesthood. Although I was a little boy, I would say three things influenced me in making that choice. The first was my parents' example of love and service to God and the community. The second was the witness of our parish priest, Fr. Kevin Ikpa, who, like Jesus, loved little children and made us feel at home in the church. He encouraged us to join the altar servers' organization, and he brought one of his nephews to teach us how to serve and introduced a cultural dance in our parish. He also organized soccer competitions and prayer groups for children, popularly known as "Block Rosary," where children gathered every evening to pray the Holy Rosary in imitation of the three children – Lucy, Jacinta and Francisco – who received the apparition message of Our Blessed Mother Mary at Fatima. He told us many stories about the apparition and our Blessed Mother's invitation for us to live a holy life, make sacrifices, fast, and atonement for the sins of the whole world. Like the other children, I prayed the Rosary very fervently and desired to be holy and to live like the three little children at Fatima. The Block Rosary prayer group was a breeding ground for many vocations to the priesthood and religious life at the time, including beautiful priests like Fr. Kevin, who made the church children-friendly. Growing up as kids, the church was our second home, where we went to pray, play and socialize. We didn't have any technology, social media or the distractions most children have today. I am grateful to our Blessed Mother Mary for nurturing our faith and leading us to Christ through the praying of the Holy Rosary. I look back to those years with much nostalgia, especially in this age when sexual abuse of minors and other scandals have marred the Catholic Church's image and that of the priesthood. I pray that we may not "throw away the baby with the bathwater." We have so many wonderful priests like Fr. Kevin, whose love and affection for children contributed to making me who I am today. It would be wonderful if our Church could become a little more intentional in creating a child-friendly environment for our children at our churches and gatherings. One of the things I enjoy most in Nigeria is seeing so many children coming to the church to play and socialize with others freely, and they are also friendly with the priests. As a little child, I always enjoyed going to the church; sometimes, we were about ten children in the Father's house. Those were the best days of my life.

When it was time to write the entrance examination to enter the minor seminary, Father Kevin encouraged all the children who wanted to become priests to apply. He offered to drive us to the exam center at St. Mary's Cathedral, Okigwe. Six of us who were altar servers indicated an interest in becoming priests, and we took the exam. Out of the six, four of us passed the exam and enrolled in the minor seminary for the 1980 academic session. Eventually, only two of us became priests, not because we were more worthy or better than the others, but because of God's mercy and love. I thank God for the priests, nuns, seminarians and lay faithful who inspired me through their life of prayer, witness, preaching and loving care.

The third factor that motivated me consciously or unconsciously to enter the seminary was the suffering and pain I experienced as a child during the Nigeria-Biafra civil war. I wanted to help other people as a missionary, especially the poor and the marginalized so that they would not experience the same ordeals I went through. Coming from a family with mixed-faith expressions – Catholics, Methodists, Pentecostals, Jehovah's Witnesses, etc., my decision to become a priest at the age of thirteen was questioned. Given our collectivist culture, I couldn't make such a decision alone. Hence, a family meeting was convened, and all my aunts and uncles were invited. They wanted to find out my reasons for choosing to be a priest, and they tried to make me understand the implications. One of my uncles asked me, "Do you know that priests do not get married and they do not have children?" I replied, "Yes." Again, he asked me, "Based on our Igbo culture, do you know that if you become a priest, you will not receive any inheritance from the family's landed property or other rights and privileges because you no longer belong to the family?" I replied in the affirmative, "I do." You can imagine the image of priesthood our people had in those days that once ordained, you no longer belonged to your family; you became God's and the Church's property. That was a big sacrifice for the family and the individual. Now, I look back and ask myself, what would a thirteen-year-old child know about marriage, children and inheritance and the other questions they raised?

However, I was convinced that God was calling me to become a priest, and I desired it with all my heart. When they saw they couldn't dissuade me, the whole family agreed to support me but with the condition that I should behave well and not bring any shame on the family. In other words, I should not do anything that would warrant my expulsion, as that was seen as a disgrace or a curse at that time in my culture. I promised them that I would do my best to behave well in the seminary and to make them proud. On the 8th of September 1980, the feast of the Nativity of the Blessed Virgin Mary, I entered the Immaculate Conception Minor Seminary, Ahiake Umuahia. I was very happy in the seminary, and even though the formation was highly rigorous, I was not daunted. With the creation of the Okigwe diocese in 1981, we were moved to St. Peter's Preparatory Seminary, Ihite-Mbano, where we spent two years and then moved to St. Peter's Seminary, Okigwe.

First year in the minor seminary (Ihite-Mbano, 1981).

Everything went very well until 1984 when I was expelled from the seminary. It was a harrowing experience for me. You must be wondering, "What crime did he commit?" Well, I didn't do anything wrong. A junior student was bullying a classmate who was very small in stature. Since he could not fight back, he reported the situation to one of the teachers (the auxiliary), who told him to flog the junior student. The junior student broke my classmate's plate in the refectory and threw away his towel in anger. Again, my classmate reported what the junior student had done to the teacher. The teacher told him to deal with it as he wished. Since my classmate could not deal with the junior student, he brought the case to the class during the afternoon study hours. After he told us the story of what had happened, we all got mad at the junior student and began to discuss what type of punishment we would give him. That raised some noise in the class, which was against the seminary rules and regulations.

Coincidentally, one of the teachers was passing by our classroom. He came into the class to find out the cause of the noise and wanted someone to explain in a few words only. When the class representative could not be brief, I stood up and said, "Since you will not allow the class rep to tell you the details of the situation, please give us five minutes because what we are discussing pertains to the class." The teacher was not satisfied with my answer. He said he was going to report us to the Rector of the seminary because, according to him, we were going against the seminary rules and regulations. After he said that, all the students began to make fun of him; some were calling him names. At that moment, the bell rang to mark the end of the study hour. When we left the classroom, one of my classmates called the teacher a name he didn't like ("Ikonso" meaning "a holy cup"), and the teacher ran after the student to catch him. The boy made a sharp U-turn and, in an attempt to grab him, the teacher fell. Almost all the students witnessed his fall, which raised an uproar in the whole school. The other teachers felt we were insulting their colleague, and they asked him to report the names of those who were responsible. He gave them eight names and put my name as the "ringleader" because I had asked him to give us five minutes to discuss what pertained to the class. No one spoke to me or asked any of us for an explanation. The Rector came to the assembly the following morning and, to my great surprise, called our names. He placed the seven other students on suspension for one month and asked them to come back with their parents to write a formal undertaking that they would never misbehave again. And, for being the "ringleader," he gave me one hour to pack my belongings and leave the seminary.

That announcement sounded like a bombshell to the rest of the students and me because no one saw it coming. I felt sad and depressed as if my world had ended. My concern was not about leaving the seminary but about my family and their expectations of me. I felt I had disappointed them and had brought disgrace to myself and them. I went to an uncle who lived near the seminary and told him that I had been expelled from the seminary. He couldn't believe what I had said, so he took me back to the seminary to enquire from the Rector about the reason for my expulsion. The rector ignored him. After waiting for almost an hour without receiving any attention, my uncle took me home. When I reached home, my dad was equally surprised and wondered why I was home. I told him the same story I had told my uncle. He didn't believe I was telling the truth, and he took me back to the seminary to see the Rector. Unfortunately, the Rector refused to give him any explanation. Instead, he told my dad to find me another school, that he couldn't take me back. As my dad insisted on getting an answer, the Rector slammed the door on us and left. We waited until the secretary to the Rector came and told us to leave the office.

When we left the Rector's office, I said, "To hell with God, the church and the priesthood." That was the first big turning point in my life. I entered a public high school and felt like a bird that had been released from a nest or cage. I "grew wings," abandoned my faith and joined a bad boys' group. Suffice it to say that I lived a rebellious life and did what every other teenager did – partying, drinking, smoking, dating, keeping late nights, etc. God was no longer part of my life. My mom was always crying and praying the rosary for my conversion. Sometimes, she would not go to bed until she knew that I was back home. She tried to advise me on several occasions, but I never listened to her. However, she never gave up on me. Each time I was about to go out, she would call me and pray for me. At the end of the prayer, she would give me her blessing and ask my guardian angel to protect me. She would always pray aloud so that I could hear what she was saying. One day she prayed, "Lord, since my son is no longer listening to me, please send an angel or someone in his life to speak to him in a language he will understand." God did answer that prayer, as will be seen later. I thank God for my mother and her prayers for me. I owe my conversion to her prayers and the intercession of our Blessed Mother Mary. My conversion story and experience will be shared later in chapter four. I love my mother and the Blessed Virgin Mary with all my heart, as they have protected me and helped me all my life.

Perhaps there is someone out there reading this book who is hurting or angry because they may have been disappointed by God, the priests, or the Church. I would like you to know that I can identify with you because I felt the same way. But thank God, I was healed from those hurts and anger when I gave my life back to Jesus. So, I encourage you to give it all to Jesus and ask him for the grace to forgive, for healing and peace. It is liberating to forgive and surrender all our emotional wounds and hurts to Christ. Only he can free us from the baggage and hang-ups we carry, which weigh us down. He says in Matthew 11:28, "Come to me all you who are weary and overburdened, and I will give you rest. My yoke is easy and my burden light. Learn from me, for I am meek and humble of heart, and you will find rest for your souls."

During my ministry as a priest, I have encountered many parents and guardians who are worried and are crying because their children or wards have abandoned their faith or made wrong choices. I tell such parents or guardians, "Instead of worrying about your children or fighting with them, it would be fantastic if you could pray the Rosary and intercede for your children. Like my mother did for me, give them your blessings and ask God to send an angel or someone to speak to them in a language they will understand. Continue to love them unconditionally and never give up on them." St. Monica prayed for the conversion of her son, Augustine, for over thirty years, and she was blessed to witness the conversion of her son, who today is a great Saint. Through prayer, the Holy Spirit can break all hardened hearts and fill them with God's love and true joy. God is always at work in our lives, and he eventually uses each experience for his glory if we look at it from his perspective.

Suggested action: Take a moment to reflect on your birth circumstances, vocation, and life experiences. Where do you see God's hand in them?

Prayer: Dear God, thank you for the gift of my life, my vocation, and the different circumstances of my life. Some experiences are wonderful and pleasant, but some are painful and sad. Please open my eyes of faith to see you at work in every circumstance of my life, and may each experience draw me closer to you, to my family and other people. Amen!

3

God works in mysterious ways

"Therefore, I say to you, walk according to the Spirit, and do not give way to the desires of the flesh. For the desires of the flesh are against the Spirit, and the desires of the Spirit are opposed to the flesh. Both are in conflict with each other, so that you cannot do everything you would like to. But let the Spirit lead you, and then you are not under the law" (Galatians 5:16-18 - NCB).

When I finished high school, I was very fortunate to pass the final exam known as WAEC (West African Examination Council). By God's grace and mercy, I had an excellent result. Out of the sixty-four students in our class who wrote the English Language exam that year, I was the only one who passed. Passing that exam was a requirement to enter the university. I must confess that I was not the most intelligent in my class but, looking back now, I know it was God who providentially helped me to pass that exam because he already knew I was not ready to repeat the exam and would need it in the future to re-enter the seminary.

With such a good result, I wanted to study Law or Business Administration at the university. Unfortunately, I failed the entrance examination to the university known as JAMB (Joint Admission and Matriculation Board). Ironically, some of my classmates passed JAMB and failed the English Language Exam. I was angry and wondered why I should pass WAEC and fail JAMB? My parents and uncles encouraged me to retake the exam, but I refused, saying, “I will never repeat any exam in my life.” I was rebellious toward any authority figure at that time because they reminded me of the seminary and the unjust treatment I had received from the Rector. Today, I would say that my failure to pass that exam was “a blessing in disguise” because, if I had passed it and entered the university, I might have joined an occult group since I was already gravitating towards a disordered and rebellious life during high school. And . . perhaps I would not be a priest today.

When my family could not convince me to retake the entrance examination to the university, they asked me what I would like to do. I told them that I would like to go into business, to learn how to trade pharmaceutical products. In those days, people who engaged in that business made a lot of money. With the help of one of my uncles, the family found a drugstore (called a chemist shop) where I could serve as an apprentice to learn the trade. I spent one year learning about drugs and different pharmaceutical products. During my year of apprenticeship and subsequent involvement in the pharmaceutical business, I experienced the dark side of the world, which St. Paul in Galatians 5 referred to as the “spirit of the flesh.” I could say, “I have seen it all.” The man I served ran a clandestine abortion clinic. Neither my parents nor my uncle knew about the man’s involvement in such a horrible practice before they arranged for me to stay with him. On two occasions, when my master was preparing to perform an abortion, he asked me to clean and set up the room and hold the light for him during the procedure. I must confess that this was against my will but, since I was an apprentice, I could not refuse since an apprentice has no freedom or rights in Nigeria. The apprentice must do whatever the master says or he will be dismissed and whatever money has been paid to him will be lost. Even though I was not practicing my faith at that time, my heart bled when I saw how the girls cried and screamed because of the excruciating pain. When it was over, most of them felt exhausted and depressed. I know that my master never explained to them the consequences the procedure might have on them physically, emotionally and spiritually. I believe, had they known, some of them would not have gone through with it. It was heartbreaking for me. Unfortunately, there was nothing I could do to stop it and, as a young boy, there was no way I could have challenged my master or walked away from there.

When I decided to enter the seminary, I discussed the experiences with my Spiritual Director and no question of irregularity was raised because I was not directly involved in the abortions and it was not a willful act on my part to be present during the procedures; I was obliged by my master to be there. That experience made me more empathetic towards girls and women who have committed abortion in the past and the men who assisted them. Because I witnessed those two procedures, I can understand what these women have gone through and, as a priest, I pray for their forgiveness and healing and try to give such women words of encouragement and hope.

Often, after confession, counselling and prayer, some women who have committed abortion experience renewed peace, life, and the joy they had lost after the procedure. They feel as if a load has been lifted off their shoulders. I remember encountering a girl feeling very sad and depressed because she had aborted her baby in high school. Many years after the incident, she was still feeling guilty. Every day she imagined her baby was speaking to her, and she could no longer bear the pain. If she saw a baby, she would say, "If I had had my baby, he or she would have been like this boy/girl." It was haunting her so severely that she was considering suicide but was terrified of the negative impact it would have on her parents and family. So, she decided to come and talk about it. Given the experience I had in the past, I understood to some extent what she was going through. I empathized with her, counselled her and gave her hope. After going to Confession and receiving absolution, she felt relieved and began to live a normal life again. She experienced God's merciful love and forgiveness through the Sacrament of Reconciliation.

I believe God must have allowed me to experience all those ugly situations in the past because he already knew that it would enable me to help some of the people who would come to me in the future for ministration. I do not claim to be a good person because I know I am not. I am still a sinner with many weaknesses and limitations but, like St. Paul, I see the strength of God's power in my weakness. Because I am weak, I can connect with different people as I have had similar experiences. I can understand young people or those who say they no longer believe in God or organized religion; I was once like them. I can appreciate those angry at God or the Church because of the scandals or failures of the leadership or some members of the Church; I've been there too. I can connect with parents who worry about their children because they have abandoned their faith or are making wrong choices that will lead to destruction; I saw my mom worry and cry for me like them. I can understand prisoners who committed crimes and those detained innocently; the latter was my experience. I can connect with people struggling in life, the sick and the needy; my mom was like them. I can connect with those living in the flesh because I am one of them. Often, I have made resolutions and vowed not to commit sin but find myself doing the very opposite. Even though I pray constantly, I still experience constant conflict between the spirit of the flesh and that of God. This has made me more restrained when passing judgment on others since I am not perfect myself. From my experiences, I realize that God can use any instrument to touch hearts and draw people closer to him; it can be within the Church or outside of the Church. God can still encounter you at the appointed time whether you are searching for him or not. It gives me hope and comfort to know that our God is a God of second chances, a God of new opportunities. There is nothing we can do to make him love us more or less. There is no sin he cannot forgive. The only thing he needs from us is to acknowledge our sins, humbly confess them and surrender to the Holy Spirit for, under his protection, there is no condemnation.

For anyone who may have committed abortion or supported it, I encourage you to forgive yourself and go to Confession, trusting in God's love and mercy. He will forgive you and will no longer remember your sins, for he said in Isaiah, "Come now, says the Lord, let us reason together. Though your sins are like scarlet, they will be as white as snow; though they are red as crimson, they will become like wool" (Isaiah 1:18 – NCB). Pray for aborted children and see them as angels in heaven. If you like, give them a name and, when negative thoughts come to accuse you, remind yourself that you have a child in heaven. Instead of carrying the weight of the guilt, give it all to the crucified Jesus and you will feel the healing balm of the Holy Spirit. Living through that experience helped me to understand St. Paul when he says that there is always a war going on in us between the flesh and the spirit. "For what the flesh desires is opposed to the Spirit, and what the Spirit desires is opposed to the flesh, for these are opposed to each other, to prevent you from doing what you want" (Galatians 5:16-22). All that the flesh produces in us leads to death but what comes from the Spirit gives life, true freedom and lasting joy. Even if we have lived in the flesh in the past, if we turn to the Lord and ask for his mercy, he will forgive us and never remind us of our sins. For "nothing will be able to separate us from the love of God in Christ Jesus our Lord" (Romans 8:39 - NCB) – not even our sins nor the devil.

Suggested action: Read Galatians 5:16-22 and take a moment to reflect on the fruits of the spirit and the flesh. To which side do you gravitate?

Prayer: Lord Jesus, you invite us to walk by the spirit and to not gratify the desires of the flesh. You know that we are weak, and it is challenging to follow the promptings of the Spirit. Please give us your grace to overcome our weaknesses and may nothing ever separate us from you. Amen!

4

Detention that led to conversion

"For my thoughts are not your thoughts, and my ways are not your ways, says the Lord. For as the heavens are higher than the earth, so are my ways higher than your ways and my thoughts above your thoughts" (Isiah 55: 8-9 - NCB).

When I finished my apprenticeship, my family raised some money and gave it to me so that I could start my own business. I lived at Onitsha but would sometimes go to the North (Kano and Kaduna) or to the West (Lagos) to buy medicine/pharmaceutical products and return home to sell them wholesale at Head-bridge Market, Onitsha. The business was flourishing, and I was making a good profit. As a young man making money, I was pleased and continued to live a disordered life, far from God and with a deep hatred for the Church and the priests.

Things suddenly changed during one of my business trips. I had gone to Kano in the North to buy some drugs: Tramadol and Gentamycin injections. The asking price seemed to be an excellent deal, given the costs at Onitsha when I left. Unfortunately, on my return, I discovered that those who had gone to Lagos to purchase the same drugs got them cheaper, arrived back home before me and flooded the market with their goods. The price difference was such that I could not compete with them. I decided to wait until they had finished selling their stock.

Meanwhile, a customer in the North requested that I supply him with some drugs. I used the money I had to buy the goods and travelled to give the customer his order. On reaching his shop, I was told that he had gone home for a funeral, and no one knew when he was returning. In those days, there was no phone to communicate with him. I tried to sell the product to other people, but they underpriced it. After spending three days in a hotel, I decided to return home with the goods. I boarded the train going from Kaduna to Enugu this time, as it was less expensive.

On arriving at Kafanchan, which was midway to my destination, two police officers checking tickets on the train approached my seat. They saw the goods I was carrying and asked who the owner was. I replied, "They are mine." The police officers asked for the receipt, the waybill and the train ticket. I provided the receipts and waybill but not the ticket. They said, "Settle us," which meant that I should bribe them. I replied, "Why should I settle you?" They answered, "Because you are carrying contraband goods". I told them that the goods were legally imported into the country and that I could not give them any money because I had already incurred a significant loss on that trip. They said that if I didn't settle them, they would drop me at the nearest police station and make a claim. I would be forced to go to court and prove that I was not carrying contraband goods. I thought they were joking, but I was wrong. When we arrived at Otukpo railway station, they forced me to get off the train with my goods and handed me over to the police to be taken to court. It was on a Friday and, since I was travelling alone, there was no one to post bail. The officers told me they could not hold me at the railway station and they were going to detain me in a nearby prison until Monday, when they would charge me in court.

The second turning point in my life, which eventually led to my conversion, happened when I arrived at Otukpo prison. Before entering the detention room, I handed over my wallet and other items I was carrying to the security officer on duty as required by their regulations. I had about ₦250 (naira) in my wallet. That was a significant amount at the time, and the police officer had been asking me for just ₦5, but I had refused. St. Augustine talked about the permissive will of God. So, I guess God permitted that I refuse to give a bribe to the police because he already had a plan to touch my heart in the prison. God's ways are not our ways; his thoughts are not our thoughts.

On entering the cell, I saw over sixty men in a room about twenty-by-twenty-four feet, and all were awaiting trial. Some of them had spent over three years in detention without their cases being heard in court. There was only one toilet in the room, which meant the inmates had not taken a bath for those days, months, and years. You can imagine the odour oozing out from them and the toilet. Once I entered the cell and inhaled that disgusting odour, I lost any appetite I may have had. I was in detention for three days, from Friday to Sunday. I did not eat, drink, sleep or take a bath for those three days. It was like hell on earth; it was my calvary.

The cell inmates had an organized quasi-political structure; there was a president, vice president, public relations officer who enforced order, etc. To my great surprise, the cell president called for night prayers on the Friday night I arrived, and some of the inmates joined him to pray. Bear in mind that it had been over four years since I left the seminary and consequently the Church, so God was not part of my life; I was living a disordered life. I didn't join them in prayer but simply observed them. When they finished praying, the president called me over and asked me what offence I had committed. I told him, and then he said, "You have no problem; you will leave here on Monday. Please pray for me when you leave because I have been here so long." I said to myself, "Woah! How can he be asking me to pray for him? If he knew me and the aversion I had for God and the Church at that time, he would not be asking me to pray for him."

The following morning, the president called for morning prayers and invited those who wished to pray with him. Again, I didn't join but observed from afar, as I was still angry with God. Then on Sunday morning, he organized the celebration of the Word. Many of the inmates joined in. They sang praises to God, prayed and shared the Word of God. The scripture passage he read was Jesus' admonition to his disciples on the need to remain faithful to him and his values and not to follow worldly values that may lead them to destruction. Jesus said, "The thief comes only to steal and kill and destroy. I came that they may have life and have it abundantly. I am the good shepherd. The good shepherd lays down his life for the sheep" (John 10:10-11 - NRSVB). In his reflection, the prisoner said, "When we were in the world, we had our freedom, but some of us did not know how to use it wisely. I was one of those people. I used to do drugs, get drunk, steal, rape and kill. I thought I was enjoying life, but it was the enemy, the devil, who blindfolded me and led me to commit those heinous crimes. This is where he has brought me, and I have been here for three years awaiting trial. They are still investigating all the crimes I committed. The devil has stolen, killed, and destroyed my life and relationship with my family, wife, and children. I don't know how long I will be in detention awaiting trial, nor do I know how long my sentence will be, but I thank God that my stay in jail has allowed me to experience Christ and his saving grace. I believe Jesus has forgiven me, and I am now a new creature. When I am released from jail, I promise to spend the remainder of my life preaching the Good News of Christ, especially to the young people, so that they don't make the same mistakes I made. Some of you here are innocent, but some of you have committed crimes like me. No matter what your past may have been, I invite you to decide about your life and future. If you have not accepted Christ in your life, I invite you to permit Jesus to come to you. Surrender your life to him because he is the only one who can give us the true and lasting happiness that we are seeking. The enemy leads to destruction, but Christ leads to life."

As he was preaching, I felt he was talking directly to me because my lifestyle included some of the vices he mentioned that lead to destruction. If there were any place I could have expected to hear the Word of God, it would never have crossed my mind that it would be in prison. If someone had told me that I would be in detention, I wouldn't have believed it… but it was so. God came to me in an unexpected place and through an unexpected person. After listening to that man preach, I said, "When I leave here, I will do something about my life."

Eventually, my mother's prayers were answered. God sent an angel, a prisoner, to speak to me in a language I could understand since I wouldn't listen to my mom or God. Now look at where my conversion story began; not in the Church nor a sacred space but in the last place one would expect to find God. No priest or church person preached to me but a prisoner. God works in mysterious ways! His ways are not our ways; his thoughts are not our thoughts. As St. Paul says, "… all things work together for good for those who love God" (Galatians 8:28 - NRSVB). I believe God allowed me to live that experience of injustice, brokenness, emptiness, poverty, hunger and thirst so that I could understand those who are broken and become an instrument to help give them hope and courage. To God be all the glory and praise, amen! When something happens in your life, and you can't make sense of it, perhaps it is not the time to ask God, "Why?" but rather, "What are you telling me, Lord?"

On Monday morning, I left the cell to go to court for my hearing. When I got to the reception counter, I asked them for the belongings that I had left there before entering the cell. I was told that the officer on duty when I entered the cell was off, and he did not record anything in the books. I insisted that they give me my money, but they told me, "Young man, the police van taking you to court is about to leave and, as your case is the first to be heard this morning, if you are called and you're not there, they will adjourn the case, and you will have to look for someone to get you out on bail. If there is no one, you will be sent back to detention." After three days of no food, drink, bath, or sleep, I did not care to know anything about the money. I hopped into the van and headed to court.

To put this in context, the police asked for ₦5, which was equivalent to about $2/3 at the time, but I refused to give it. If I had bribed them, they would have let me go and perhaps I wouldn't have had that ugly experience. But God allowed me to have the horrible experience because he already knew that it would lead to my conversion. This affirms that "There is no accident or coincidence in God's plan." There is always a reason why God allows whatever happens in your life, whether you perceive it as "good or bad." It is only with time that you will come to realize it.

On arrival at the court, the prosecutor read out all the charges against me – carrying contraband goods, insulting the police, not holding a train ticket, etc. The judge asked if I had a lawyer, and I said, "No." I was given a Bible and asked to take an oath, to tell the truth, and nothing but the truth. Then the judge asked me whether I was guilty or not. I said I was not guilty, and then she asked me to make my statement. I told her that a registered company legally imported the goods I was carrying; I had my receipts indicating where I bought them, so they were not smuggled into the country. I had a ticket, but it was lost on the train, and I hadn't insulted the police, but only refused to bribe them and when they said I was carrying contraband goods, I contradicted them. So, they said I was insulting them and that they would drop me at the nearest police station. The judge asked to be shown the exhibit and the receipts. After examining them, she said to the prosecutor, "Why did you bring this young man here; he was hustling to make a living. Give him back his goods." And she dismissed my case. My hearing did not last more than twenty minutes. God is great, just and merciful!

Fortunately, some people on the train with me knew me and my brother, Edwin. When they arrived home, they told him that I had been taken away by the police. Edwin came to the hearing and, after my release, he took me to a hotel to shower and eat. It was like a "resurrection experience." I was like Jonah, who spent three days in the belly of the fish, or Jesus who spent three days in the tomb. It was a challenging and sad experience, but it brought new purpose and perspective to my life.

Suggested action: Take a little time to think about those in the prisons or those being marginalized or discriminated against unjustly. Pray that God may help those who committed crimes to experience his mercy and conversion, healing for the victims of crimes and protection for the marginalized or those persecuted for their faith.

Prayer: Dear Jesus, thank you for answering my mother's prayers by sending someone to share the Good News of your love and mercy with me even when I was in prison. Please touch the hearts of all those in jail, whether they committed any crimes or not, whether they are justly or unjustly detained. Grant them freedom, and through their experience in prison, may you transform their lives through the power of your love and Holy Spirit. Amen!

5

I heard a voice

"As he travelled along and was approaching Damascus, a light from the sky suddenly flashed around him. He fell to the ground and heard a voice saying to him, "Saul, Saul! Why do you persecute me?" He asked, "Who are you, Lord?" The voice replied, "I am Jesus, whom you are persecuting." Now get up and go into the city, and you will be told what you are to do." The men who were travelling with him stood speechless; they heard the voice but could see no one. Saul got up from the ground but, when he opened his eyes, he could not see anything *at all*. They took him by the hand and brought him into Damascus. For three days, he was without sight, and did not eat or drink anything" (Acts 9:3-9 – NCB).

My brother invited me to spend a few days with him before returning to my home base. I readily accepted as I needed some rest after that dreadful experience in jail. The following day, being a Tuesday, before he left for his business, he gave me money to buy groceries for dinner.

I went to the market to buy food items, and on my way home, I saw a group of Block Rosary children praying the Holy Rosary. One of the boys, approximately fourteen years old, was teaching and instructing the other children about the rosary. As I passed by, I heard a voice saying, "This is what I want you to be doing, and you are out there wasting your life." I stopped and looked around, but I couldn't see anyone. It seemed like something was pinning me down, so I couldn't move. I stood there for about thirty minutes, watching the children and the boy and thinking about what I had heard. When I left there and arrived home, I became restless; I was feeling empty, and for the first time in four years, I said some prayers and grabbed my brother's Bible to read. I didn't know exactly what to read, so I opened it at random. It opened at Psalm 51 which is a prayer of repentance and pardon by King David when prophet Nathan came to rebuke him after he had committed adultery with Bathsheba and killed her husband Uriah. David prayed thus, "Have mercy on me, O God, in your unfailing love; in your abundant compassion, blot out my sin. Wash me thoroughly of my guilt; and cleanse me from my sin, for I acknowledge my wrongdoings, and my sin is always before me. Against you, you alone, have I sinned; what is evil in your sight I have done" (Psalm 51:1-3 – NCB).

I chose to quote these lines from the psalm because I could identify with St. Paul and his conversion experience. He was fighting against Christians, but from the moment he heard the voice of God and had an encounter with Jesus, his life changed, and he gave his life to preaching the Good News and bringing people to Jesus. After I heard that voice – in prison, on the street, in the church, my life was never the same. Like St. Paul, I surrendered to God and decided to give my life to preaching the Good News and bringing people to Jesus. Coincidentally, my birthday is January 25th which is the feast of the conversion of St. Paul. No mistake in God's plan!

That was just what I needed - a prayer for the forgiveness of my sins. As I prayed that psalm, my heart yearned for more. For the first time, I felt my emptiness and unworthiness and continued to read the psalms. The more I prayed, the more peaceful I felt, and I thirsted and longed to be filled. The Word of God I had heard preached by the prisoner was also a ringing bell in my head. "The enemy comes to steal, kill, and destroy, but I have come that you may have life and have it more abundantly" (John 10:10). As I read the Bible and prayed, I became more and more aware of my brokenness and emptiness.

On Sunday, I decided to go to Mass after many years of absence. The church was packed with people; the choir sang beautifully, which I enjoyed very much, and the Gospel was taken from Mt. 16:26: "For what will it profit them if they gain the whole world but forfeit their life? Or what will they give in return for their life?" In his homily, the priest preached about detachment from material things and building an intimate relationship with God because it is the only thing that lasts forever. He asked the crowd, "Do you know anyone who was very wealthy and then died?" Many said, "Yes." "Again, do you know someone very intelligent – bagged doctorate degrees and other academic awards and then died?" Everyone said, "Yes." "Do you know anyone who was very beautiful or handsome, someone very powerful or famous, who had great mansions or assets and who then died? The majority said, "Yes." And then he asked, "Did they take anything out of this world? Are they still remembered today?" Many people replied, "No." Then he said, "That is the message of today's Gospel. It would be foolish to let this world's material things or pleasures deprive you of the eternal happiness that God has prepared for those who love him." And he concluded by asking, "If you were to die today, if God called you home today, where would you spend eternity? Would you take all the wealth you have accumulated or those things that separate you from having a relationship with God? Do a self-examination today for, as Socrates said, "An unexamined life is not worth living."

As the priest was preaching, I felt that he was talking to me, just like when I was in detention and the prisoner's message seemed to be specifically meant for me. At the end of the Mass, a member of the Catholic Charismatic Renewal Movement made an announcement inviting anyone who wished to enter a deeper relationship with God to come to their evening prayer meeting and bring their rosary and Bible with them. Even though I had been to church many times before, I had never felt as good leaving Mass as I did that day. I felt uplifted by the music and inspired by the sermon to reflect on my life and redirect my priorities. I left with the desire to respond to that invitation. This is an example of how God's Word has the power to transform lives and how God can use anyone as his instrument to touch people's hearts. Sometimes we preach the Word of God, but we do not know or see the impact it has on people's lives. As the author of the letter to the Hebrews said, "The Word of God is alive and active. Sharper than any double-edged sword, it penetrates even to dividing soul and spirit, joints, and marrow; it judges the thoughts and attitudes of the heart" (Heb. 4:12).

Also, as Isaiah said, "God's word shall never return without accomplishing that for which it was sent" (Isaiah 55:11). And Jesus said, "Heaven and earth will pass away, but my Word will never pass away" (Mt. 24:35). Everything works unto good to those who love God. I am sure that neither the prisoner nor the priest had the slightest idea of what their preaching did in my heart and my life. Although the prisoner confessed to being a sinner who committed many crimes, God used him to draw me closer to him. God knew that, at that point in my life, I was not willing to listen to any priest or anyone close to me talk to me about God. He knew I was never going back to church. He knew detention was horrible, yet he inspired me to not give a bribe to the police. He knew I was innocent, but he allowed them to detain me unjustly because he knew it would bring about a turning point in my life. In detention, there was no escape. I had no choice but to listen to the preaching. If I had not been detained, I couldn't have listened. This reminds me of what happened one day…We were a group of boys hanging out together, and a girl came to preach; I was smoking and blowing the fumes in her face. I told her to get out and that she would not preach there. She begged me to allow her to preach, but I said, "No." So she had to leave but, before she left, she said to me, "You don't want me to preach about Jesus. One day, you will be preaching about him." And here I am preaching about Jesus! I bet that girl had no idea that her words were prophetic. God is the Master Planner. Therefore, when things don't work out the way you have planned, do not lose heart; wait on God, for he always has another plan, and his plan is always the best.

On the evening of that Sunday, I went to the charismatic prayer group. I took my brother's Bible with me but was very ashamed of myself and my past life. I didn't want my friends to know I was carrying a Bible, so I wrapped it in a newspaper. Eventually, some of them saw me entering the church and said, "What is this devil going to do in the church? Maybe there is a girl in the group he is going after." They didn't know what was going on in my heart: a change, a conversion, was already taking place. They judged me by what they knew about my past life and outward appearance. They had given up on me, but God never gives up on us, no matter our past. He believes in us, and he gives us new opportunities to come back to him. Like the prodigal son in Luke 15:11-32, each time we come back to God, he welcomes us with a party like the good and merciful Father. As Jesus said, "There will be more joy in heaven over one sinner who repents than over ninety-nine righteous persons who need no repentance" (Luke 15:7). So, no matter what your past may have been, you can always start anew. The members of the prayer meeting warmly welcomed me and were very happy to introduce me to the group. We prayed the rosary, sang songs of praise and worship, shared the Word of God and prayed spontaneous intercessory prayers. It was so beautiful, and I felt so happy. They encouraged us to continue reading the Bible and to make time for personal prayer and meditation each day for at least fifteen minutes. They recommended starting the day by attending daily Mass if possible. I left with more hunger and thirst for God. I started reading the New Testament. The Bible began to feel so tasty and sweet; I couldn't stop reading and praying. It was so soothing to my soul. I then understood what the Psalmist meant when he said, "Taste and see, that the Lord is good" (Ps. 34:8). Before leaving my brother's house that week, my faith was reignited, and I had already made up my mind to go back fully to the Church. I've never forgotten those voices.

Suggested action: Do you want to grow in your relationship with Jesus? I suggest you join a prayer group or connect with a group if you are not in one already. Or select a few friends with whom you can pray and share the Word of God. If you have questions about life and faith, you can take the ALPHA course or watch "The Search" on Formed.org or YouTube. You can also talk to a priest or spiritual counsellor.

Prayer: Dear Jesus, help me to know that the most important thing that will last forever is friendship with you. May this world's material things or pleasures never separate me from you. Be the center of my life and help me love you and all your people. Amen!

6

God can make a way where there seems to be none

> "But now, thus says the Lord, he who created you, O Jacob, he who formed you, O Israel: Fear not, for I have redeemed you; I have called you by your name, you are mine. When you pass through the waters, I will be with you; when you pass through the rivers, they will not sweep you away. When you walk through fire, you will not be burned, nor will the flames consume you. For I am the Lord, your God, the Holy One of Israel, your Saviour… Since you are precious in my sight, since you are important and I love you, I give people in exchange for you, and nations in return for your life. Fear not, for I am with you; I will bring your children from the east and gather you from the west… You are my witnesses, says the Lord, you are my servant whom I have chosen, so that you may know and believe me and understand that I am He…" (Isaiah 43:1-10 – NCB).

When I returned home, I inquired about the parish nearest to where I lived, and I was directed to Iba Pope, Awada. The parish priest, Father Anthony Igweagu, was a wonderful eloquent preacher, very charismatic, loving and caring. While I was at the 5 a.m. morning Mass, he challenged every parishioner to identify their spiritual gifts and talents and use them to serve God in any ministry in the parish. I remembered the voice I heard: "This is what I want you to be doing, and you are out there in the world wasting your life." Since I was an ex-seminarian, I decided to become an altar server and help organize the Block Rosary children. As a great preacher, Fr. Anthony received a lot of invitations to speak at conferences or parish retreats. He would often invite some of us to accompany him. I always enjoyed going with him because I longed to be fed by the Word of God and couldn't get enough of it. The more I listened to him, the more I desired to become a priest, but I thought it would not be possible since I had been expelled from the minor seminary.

One day in his homily, Father Anthony challenged us to go to the Benedictine monastery at Awhum, Enugu State, to see how the monks live a life of prayer and total surrender to God because they want to go to heaven. I took on that challenge and went.

When I arrived at the monastery, I felt so much peace that I desired to remain there for good. It was like having the type of experience Peter, James and John had during the transfiguration when Peter had a glimpse of the glory of God and wanted to remain there forever (Mt. 17:4). At that time in my conversion journey, the only thing that gave me peace and joy was the Word of God and prayer. I saw myself detaching from many things that had given me joy in the past – drinks, women and parties. I had to call my girlfriend and tell her it was over. I loved her a lot, and she loved me too, but my new love experience with the Lord Jesus was more powerful. I even went to the extent of giving her back all her pictures because looking at them reminded me of the past. She cried a lot and begged me not to leave her or, at least, keep her photographs, but I said no because I didn't want her to be a distraction to me on my new journey. I know I broke her heart, and I apologized to her years later. I was very immature then and didn't know how to handle the separation gently. I am sure that, if it were now, I would have done it differently. Now, I have some understanding of how those going through broken relationships feel; it really hurts. I am glad that my friend is happily married today with three children; she has forgiven me and is happy that I am a priest. She always prays for me and for the success of my ministry.

Given the beautiful experience at the monastery, I told the Abbot that I would like to join them. He asked me, "What type of people do you think you will find in the monastery?" I replied, "People who have given their lives to God and are dedicated to a life of prayer." He said, "Suppose you enter and discover that some of the monks are not as prayerful or holy as you thought because they are still human beings with human weaknesses and limitations, what will you do?" I told him that I was not looking at any human being as my model at this point in my faith journey. "Only Jesus Christ is perfect, and only he is my model. If I enter the monastery, I will focus my gaze on him, not on any monk. Jesus is my only motivation for coming here and nothing more." After asking me some other questions and having other conversations with me, he was impressed with my responses, and he said, "Young man, the way I see you, you will be more useful to God in the world than in the monastery. So, I advise you to go and look for a religious community of active life. But, if you can't find one after six months, you can come back, and we will accept you." He then gave me some Psalms to pray every day (Psalms 32, 51, 60, 65, 85, 91 and 117). When I had finished speaking with him, I went to the chapel and knelt before the Blessed Sacrament. I prayed to Jesus, "Dear Lord, you have heard what the Abbot said. If you don't want me to come back here, please open another door for me."

I still needed to support myself, but at this time, my business was already at a standstill, and I didn't have enough money to make another business trip while waiting to sell my goods. So, when I left the monastery, I went to my uncle, Dr. Obi Theophilus Egbeocha, who was at that time a lecturer at the University of Nigeria Nsukka, to ask him for a loan to boost my business. He asked me what had happened to my money? I told him how my money was tied up in my goods and that I needed more money to continue making a turnover. He said, "If I see your goods, I will burn them to ashes." I asked him, "Why?" He replied, "Because I want you to go to the university. You know that education is power. If you want to go into business, you should study business administration. He gave me the example of a wealthy businessman in my town who entered politics and won the election to represent his community in the House of Assembly. Though he was wealthy, he could not represent his people well because he was not able to express himself competently in the English language.

After his four-year term in politics, he went to the university to study law though he was already in his late fifties. He said to me, "If you are educated, no one can take away your knowledge and you can easily get a job anywhere. Your goods are now unavailable and you have no money. If you have an education and armed robbers attack you and steal your money, you may lose everything but can start life afresh."

He encouraged me to retake the entrance examination to the university or go back to the seminary to become a priest. It might interest you to know that at that time, my uncle was not a Catholic, though he later converted to Catholicism. I told him that I would not repeat the exam and that I would like to go back to the seminary to become a priest, but it was almost impossible for them to take me back since I had been expelled. He said he had a priest friend who was a professor at the university and a missionary priest. He gave me three days to pray and make up my mind. At the end of the three days, I confirmed my desire to become a priest if they would take me back. Otherwise, I would continue with my business. He took me to the priest, who gave me the address of the Vocational Director of the Spiritan Religious Congregation and gave me directions to his residence. On my way, I stopped by the Bigard Memorial Seminary to visit a friend who told me about the Claretian missionaries. He suggested I try them too and wait for whichever called me first. I sent an application to both congregations.

Usually, courses for new postulants start in September but, as God would have it, the Claretian Missionaries wanted to separate first-year classes for postulants, which had included Philosophy, from classes for other students of Philosophy. Because of that change, they had to take two batches of new admissions in the same year so that half would start in April to fill the gap. Remember that the Abbot at the monastery had given me six months to find a religious community with an active life. The six months would have been up in June. Two weeks later, I submitted my application. The Claretians called me for an orientation session and later for an interview. One interesting incident during the interview was that one of the priests in the five-person panel asked me why I wanted to be a Claretian missionary and not join my home diocese? I told him that I had attended a minor seminary in my diocese for over three years but that I had been expelled. He was surprised to hear that and asked me why? I told him about my experience, and he asked who the rector was. When I told him, he said, "I know him; he is a very erratic man who destroyed many vocations. And because you told the truth, I will accept you. You do not need to continue with the interview."

Out of sixty-four candidates who applied, eighteen were admitted, and I was one of them. I learned from that experience that it pays to be honest. Also, when you experience failures or setbacks in your business or work life, do not get discouraged; be attentive because God may be opening a new door. Often, we get caught up in our failures or closed doors and fail to see the new opportunities ahead. I would say God froze my business so that he might turn my attention to the new calling he had chosen for me. If my business had been going well and I hadn't been stopped by the police or put in detention, perhaps I wouldn't have heard his voice.

In 1989, I became a postulant with the Claretian Missionaries at Enugu. Later, I attended a one-year Novitiate Formation program followed by four years of Philosophy and four years of Theology. I was ordained a priest in 1998 at the age of thirty-one. I thank God that my mum witnessed my conversion and priestly ordination, though she was very sick at the time. She died a year later. Fortunately, a week before she died, I went to visit her. She was so excited to see me. After our conversation, she went to Confession with me. After that, I prayed for her, and she prayed for me and gave me her blessing. We said our goodbyes, and I left. I saw some ladies from my village as I was going, and I stopped to greet them. Suddenly, I saw my mum running after me. I approached her and asked what she needed. She said she needed nothing; she just wanted to give me a blessing.

I was surprised because she had just prayed for me before I left her a few minutes before. She said, "My son, before you came into this world, it was God who gave you life and gave you to me. We gave you the name Toochukwu, which means "Praise God," and you have accepted giving your life to praise God and serve him and his people. You will go to many places as a missionary, and wherever you go, God will be with you, and the people will love you. Even if you don't have anything to give to the people, give them your smile and love. May God bless you and may our Blessed Mother Mary watch over you in the name of the Father and the Son and the Holy Spirit." She made a sign of the cross on my forehead and said to me, "My son, I am now happy. I would have been very sad if you had left before I had the opportunity to do this. You can now go in peace." Little did I know that would be the last blessing I would receive from her. She died a week after that encounter. God answered her prayers, and her blessings have always followed me everywhere I go. My mum prayed so much for my conversion. She trusted in God, and she was not disappointed. How wonderful it is to learn to trust God in all things and pray with the conviction that he will answer us, even when we do not see any obvious signs. It is wonderful when parents bless their children, especially before they leave the house or during their last days on earth. I suggest that parents pray for their children; pray aloud so that your children will hear you express your heart's desires. Remember that your word has power. I still remember most of those things my mom said. She thought I was not listening, but it was registering. That corroborates this quote a friend sent to me, "We cannot force someone to hear a message they are not ready to receive. However, we must never underestimate the power of planting a seed."

Suggested action: Make a list of your loved ones who have stopped practicing their faith; write them a letter or send a card to remind them you love them and that God loves them. Encourage them to get back to church and invite them to your parish mission or retreat.

Prayer: Lord Jesus, I present to you all my loved ones and those who have dropped out of church for one reason or another. Send your Holy Spirit to renew them and fill their hearts with the desire to turn back to you. Amen!

7

Miracles of healing still happen

> "Go into all the world and proclaim the good news to the whole of creation. The one who believes and is baptized will be saved; the one who does not believe will be condemned. These signs will accompany those who believe. In my name they will cast out demons, they will speak new tongues, they will pick up snakes in their hands, and if they drink any deadly thing, it will not hurt them; they will lay their hands on the sick, and they will recover… And the apostles went out and proclaimed the good news everywhere, while the Lord worked with them and confirmed the message by the signs that accompanied it" (Mark 16:15-20 - NCB).

In Mark's Gospel, we read that before Jesus ascended into heaven, he gave his apostles this great commission. Christ desires that his good news and merciful love be proclaimed to all nations. The mandate to go and make disciples of all nations did not end with the apostles. We have also been sent to go and share our faith and God's love with others by our baptism. We have been sent to go and heal the sick, expel demons, and give hope to the world. The same Jesus who used the apostles as his instrument of miraculous healing is still using many men and women today to show his healing love and mercy to his people. Though unworthy, I have been privileged to witness this healing love and mercy.

As a seminarian and priest, I have experienced many miraculous healings. Notwithstanding my sins, brokenness and woundedness, God has used me as his instrument of healing and merciful love. I would like to share some of those testimonies with you, just like the Apostles shared their testimonies of what God did in their lives and through them. Please note that sharing these testimonies is not meant to draw attention to myself but to give God thanks, praise, and glory for his goodness and mercy to me and those to whom I minister. As Psalm 144 says, "Your friends, O Lord, shall make known the glorious splendour of your reign. All your creatures shall thank you, O Lord, and your friends shall repeat your blessings. They shall speak of the glory of your reign and declare your might, O God, to make known to men your mighty deeds and the glorious splendour of your reign." The sharing of your testimonies is one way of joining the Psalmist in acknowledging the mighty deeds of God in your life. It is also meant to give hope and encouragement to those experiencing any struggle, pain or disappointment in life so they know that, in the name of Jesus Christ, they can be well again, because God is with them; they are not alone. The Bible is a record of the experiences the Israelites and the early Christians had in their faith and life journey with God. Can you imagine what Christianity would have looked like if the Apostles or early Christians had not written or shared the testimonies about their encounter with Jesus Christ and what Jesus did in and through them? Perhaps we wouldn't have the Bible today. So, I invite you to write the testimony of the good things God is doing in your life and share it with others. That way, you give glory to your Father in heaven. Remember it is not about you and me, it is about Jesus. If one person is encouraged to grow closer to Jesus after listening to your testimony, you will have done a great work for God. You cannot underestimate the value of one soul because, for the salvation of one soul, Jesus is willing to die on the cross again and again. Like the good shepherd, he is willing to leave the 99 in search of the one person who has lost his or her way (Luke 15:4). The Holy Spirit will help us to respond to our mission and share our testimony for the glory of God and the salvation of souls.

The Holy Spirit is real

One of the mysteries I have always quietly pondered in my mind is the mystery of the Holy Spirit. I had heard about the Holy Spirit from childhood and learned about him in catechism class, but I had never felt his presence until 1993 when I was in my third year of studying Philosophy. Although I became a member of the Catholic Charismatic movement after my conversion, before my personal experience with the outpouring of the Holy Spirit, I was very skeptical when I saw people speaking in tongues or crying when they were praying or when there were manifestations of some of the gifts of the Holy Spirit – such as prophecy, vision, healing, resting in the Spirit, etc. I always thought that people were pretending or making things up. I had called members of other Christian denominations or members of the Catholic

Charismatic movement who spoke of those gifts, "crazy-matics."

There was a Catholic Charismatic movement in the seminary, and I was part of the group. Once, we had a Life in the Spirit seminar – a seven-week spiritual exercise aimed at helping individuals discover all the spiritual gifts that God wants to give through the Holy Spirit to find a deeper life in God and a new life in the Spirit. One of the Life in the Spirit Seminar topics is "Baptized in the Spirit." During that session, participants are prayed over for a fresh outpouring of the Holy Spirit and his seven-fold gifts. Each person is asked to pray for a specific gift or fruit of the Holy Spirit that they want. The seven gifts of the Holy Spirit are wisdom, knowledge, understanding, counsel, fortitude, piety and fear of God or reverence for God. Other gifts include prophecy, gifts of healing, speaking in tongues, interpretation of tongues, faith, miracles, discernment of Spirits, etc. The fruit of the Spirit is love, joy, peace, patience, kindness, generosity, faithfulness, gentleness and self-control. Some of my colleagues prayed for the gift of tongues, healing, etc. I simply said in my heart, "Holy Spirit, please help me love like Jesus." When the priest prayed over me, I felt peace within me and inner joy. At the end of the prayers, we sang some praises to God, and after that, I continued to sing praises to God all day. It was a joy that I could not contain.

The Feast of Pentecost was a free day when seminarians were allowed to go outside the seminary to visit family and friends. One of my friends invited me to visit his family with him on that Feast Day. After the visit, we saw a group of charismatics gathered in his local parish to celebrate Pentecost on our way back to the seminary. My friend belonged to that group, so he suggested we go and say hi to his friends there, about forty of them in number. After exchanging pleasantries with the group, they requested that we pray for them before leaving. My friend prayed for them and later began to lay hands on them. Since they were many, he asked me to help him out. That was the first time I prayed over people. To my great surprise, when I laid my hands on the first person, he fell, which is called in the charismatic parlance, "Resting in the Spirit."

I prayed for the second person, and she fell as well, and so did all the people I prayed over. They were all lying on the floor. I couldn't believe what I was seeing. It was then that I knew that the Holy Spirit is REAL, that the people were not pretending. It was an outpouring of the Holy Spirit. Some people spoke in tongues, and some felt peace and joy and praised God as I had done when I was prayed over. My joy knew no bounds, and I sang praises to God throughout the journey. At that moment, I saw the words of Jesus in Mark's gospel become fulfilled: "These signs will accompany those who believe, in my name they will speak new tongues…" (Mk. 16:17-18). It was then that I realized that we don't have to know it all nor become perfect for the Holy Spirit to fill us or use us for God's glory. Thank you, Holy Spirit, for your seven-fold gifts and your fruits. Please continue to lead us to Jesus and the Father. Continue to renew our hearts and fill us with your love, peace and joy. And thank you,

Jesus, for confirming your word and using us as your instruments despite our unworthiness. Whenever you see someone sick or in any kind of need, I encourage you to pray for the person. It doesn't have to be a long prayer. Just rely on the promises of Jesus, who said, "In my name, you shall lay your hands on the sick, and they will be healed" (Mk. 16:17-18) and say whatever you wish for the person. There is power in the Name of Jesus, and he always fulfills his promises.

My son, your prayers have saved me

The first miraculous healing I experienced was when, as a seminarian, I was sent on apostolic work to Ebe in the Enugu Diocese. During the six weeks of missionary experience, I organized morning prayers and catechism classes to prepare children for the sacraments of First Holy Communion and Confirmation to be celebrated at the end of the mission. After one of our morning prayers, a lady came to me and requested that I visit her dad, who was sick. I took three young children from the catechism group to see the man. When we arrived, he was lying down unconscious on his bed. I didn't know what to do. I invited the children to pray the Rosary with me, followed by the Divine Mercy Chaplet and spontaneous prayers. In the end, I sprinkled Holy Water around the room and said to his wife, "Everything will be alright; we have commended him to the loving hands of God." I didn't feel anything during the prayers; I just said that to comfort his wife.

Meanwhile, his daughter had gone to look for a taxi to take the man to the hospital. As we were leaving, I asked his wife to let me know if he needed the Anointing of the Sick or Holy Communion so that I could inform the parish priest. I waited to hear from the family but heard nothing. The man's daughter came to morning prayer the following morning, and I asked her about her dad. She replied, "My dad is completely healed!" Wondering if she had taken him to the hospital, I asked her to tell me how he got healed so quickly. She said her dad was already well before she came back with the taxi and she asked me to see her dad so he could give me a complete account of his healing himself. After my breakfast, I took the three children who had been with me for the prayers, and we went to visit the man. As soon as we entered their house, the man jumped up and gave me a big hug saying, "My son, your prayers have saved me." I said, "Papa, what happened?" He told me to sit down. I sat down, and he said, "I had a spiritual attack the night before you came to my house. I found myself in the spiritual world where my enemies bound my hands, feet and throat; hence I could not speak nor move my body. They were digging a grave to bury me, and they had almost finished when you entered with the three little children. When you entered, three angels accompanied you. As soon as you started praying the Rosary, I began to regain my consciousness, and the evil spirits ran away. You sprinkled the Holy Water when you had finished your prayers and said to my wife, 'Everything will be alright; he is now in God's hands.' As you were leaving, one of the angels accompanying you was sent to come and loose all the bindings and set me free. I lifted my hand and saw it was free; lifted my leg, and it was free; then I got up from the bed." When my wife saw what had happened, she was astonished and began to shout and praise God. All the neighbours came to see what had happened. She gave me a glass of water to drink and some food to eat to make sure I was well. I was eating when my daughter came back in a taxi. On seeing the crowd, she began to cry, thinking that I was dead; but I had been healed miraculously, to her great surprise." I was amazed at hearing this testimony. I hadn't felt anything as we said those prayers, and I never knew that we had angels among us.

I guess this man's experience may sound like a fairy tale to most people from the Western world or those with a scientific mindset. It is scientifically absurd to think of how someone can have a spiritual attack from evil spirits or evil-minded people; however, this reality transcends scientific explanation, and many people are grappling with such problems. From my little experience in the ministry, such phenomena seem more common in Africa and South America. Regardless of where or how such problems take place, knowing that Jesus always fulfills his promises, we should turn to Him in prayer and trust him completely. He will faithfully be with us as he promised to protect us and work through us to bring his healing love and mercy to his people. The greatest weapon you have as a Christian against any form of spiritual attack or warfare is prayer and the Word of God. So, make it a habit to pray your Rosary and pray with your Bible every day. Attend Mass frequently, especially on Sunday, go to Confession and receive Jesus in the Eucharist at least once a week.

Healing of a paralyzed boy

In many passages of the New Testament, we read about Jesus or the disciples healing many with different kinds of sicknesses, including the lame and the blind. For example, in Mat. 19:1-8, Jesus healed a paralyzed man who was brought to him by his friends. Seeing that they couldn't get to Jesus because he was surrounded by the crowd, they climbed the house, opened the roof and dropped the lame man in front of Jesus. When he saw their faith, he forgave the sins of the paralyzed man and healed him. Also, at the pool of Bethesda, Jesus healed an undeserving crippled man telling him, "Take up your mat and go" (John 5:1-16). In Acts of the Apostles 3:6, we read the story of the healing of a crippled man at the beautiful gate who was begging for alms. Peter said to him, "Silver or gold I do not have, but what I do have I give you. In the name of Jesus Christ of Nazareth, rise up and walk." And the man got up and walked, praising God.

These healing miracles seemed to be idle tales until I experienced a boy, paralyzed from birth, begin to walk. It happened this way. In February 2000, two years after my ordination, I worked as an associate pastor at St. Paul's Parish, Nekede, Owerri. The charismatic prayer group of my parish organized a revival to begin the year. We invited a guest speaker, Fr. Innocent, who was very gifted and under a powerful anointing of the Holy Spirit. There was a very large crowd in attendance, so the event was held outdoors. After the opening Mass, the priest exposed the Blessed Sacrament and preached about the healing power of the name of Jesus. At the end of his sermon, he began to minister to the people and call out to those who needed healing prayers for different illnesses. While he was speaking, many young people made noise and distracted those praying. So, I appealed to them to leave the church premises if they were unwilling to join in the prayers. As I was going toward the young people, the priest asked me to come and assist him in praying for the people as their number was so great. I went and joined him in praying for the people.

I came upon one little boy who was about six years old. I discovered that he was crippled and his mother had brought him for prayers and left him before the Blessed Sacrament. I asked the mother what the problem was, and she said, "He is six years old and unable to walk." I didn't know what to do. I just placed my hands on the little boy and looked at Jesus in the Blessed Sacrament and I said, "Lord Jesus, I believe that you are present in the Blessed Sacrament. You made the deaf to hear, the mute to speak, and the lame to walk. Please heal this boy for the glory of your name." Then I gave my hands to the little boy and said, "In the name of Jesus, rise and walk." And immediately, the little boy got up and walked. It was a miracle! All glory, praise and thanksgiving be to our Lord Jesus Christ. I couldn't believe what I was seeing. The little boy's mother shouted, jumping up, singing and praising God. When the whole crowd saw what had happened, they joined in singing and praising God. It was unbelievable to see the many miracles of healing that night. The entire arena was set on fire with praises and dancing in thanksgiving to God for his mighty deeds. I was amazed and humbled by what God can do. He continues to heal today using weak and unworthy human instruments. So never be afraid to pray for physical or spiritual healing either for yourself or for others. You never know how and when God will answer. Let us have an expectant faith and trust in the healing mercy of God.

Suggested Action: Visit someone sick or give them a call. If you are comfortable, say some prayers with the person and ask Jesus to bring healing where it is needed most. You can simply say, "In the name of Jesus, I claim healing for… (insert the name of the person)."

Prayer: Lord Jesus, you promised that the sick would be healed in your name. Please fulfill your promises and use me as your instrument to bring healing to those who are sick for the glory of your name and the salvation of souls. Amen!

8

Colombia:
an experience of love and miracles

"The thief comes only to steal, kill and destroy. I have come so that you might have life and have it in all its fullness" (John 10:10).

Love: the universal language

After the revival experience, I was sent as a missionary to Colombia. Since Colombia didn't have a consulate in Nigeria at the time, I went to Madrid, Spain, to process my visa to Colombia. I went with three other colleagues. That was my first trip outside of Africa; suffice to say, it was a remarkable experience. Although we studied Spanish in the seminary, it was very elementary, and, as students, most of us didn't pay much attention to the class. We just studied enough to pass our exams since it was part of our curriculum. My colleagues and I knew nothing in Spanish, so we could not communicate. Thankfully, one of our veteran missionaries, Anistus, who was travelling with us, spoke Spanish. He became our translator and tour guide. After almost three months in Madrid, my colleagues and I left for our mission land; two colleagues went to Panama and two of us to Colombia. On arriving at Medellin, Colombia, we were warmly welcomed by the then provincial superior, Oscar Velez, who is now a bishop, and another priest who spoke some English. A few days after our arrival, we enrolled in a language school. It was an exciting and enriching experience to learn a new language. The people were so friendly, patient, lovely and supportive. Even when we made mistakes or couldn't express ourselves well, they laughed over it and gently corrected us. I learned that love is a universal language in Colombia, which eventually inspired me to write the song "Love, the Universal Language." The song's lyrics say, "No matter your language, no matter your colour, culture, gender or creed, everybody needs love, and everybody needs to love. Love is the language of the heart..." We all understand the language of love. That's why Jesus summarized the commandments into two – 'Love God with all your heart and love your neighbour as yourself.' The world needs a revolution of love if we want peace, happiness and unity. That song was eventually recorded, and the proceeds go to support the poor and needy in Nigeria, Colombia and Canada or wherever help is needed.

My missionary journey to Colombia is an experience I will never forget. I would say that, if not for the violence, killings and systemic corruption that generate poverty in the land, Colombia would be a paradise on earth. It is one of the most beautiful countries in the world. The people are beautiful, lovely and affectionate, and they have a great love for Jesus and our Blessed Mother Mary. As a missionary priest, I was privileged to visit many parts of Colombia where my religious order (the Claretian Missionaries) has communities, and it was a memorable experience. I still have many friends in different parts of Colombia today. I thank God for that beautiful country and its people. I pray that there may be peace and justice in the land. I experienced many miracles during my five-year mission there, of which I would like to share just a few.

God can use anything as an instrument of healing

One of the criticisms or objections some non-Catholics, especially Pentecostals, have against Catholics is that we pray through the intercession of our Blessed Mother Mary and the Saints or use sacramentals and symbols in prayer. With due respect to whatever reasons they may have, I wish to state that, as Catholics, we believe that only God can heal through Jesus and in the power of the Holy Spirit. But we cannot put God in a box nor limit him. He can use anything he has created as an instrument of healing. When we use sacramentals like Holy Water, Holy Oils, or the Crucifix to pray for the sick, it is not those objects that heal the individual, but when they are blessed, God can use them to heal as he wishes. We see that Jesus sometimes used material objects to heal, and at other times he simply said a word and the person was healed. For example, in John's gospel (John 9:6), Jesus spat on the ground, made some mud with the saliva, and put it on the blind man's eyes, and he recovered his sight.

In contrast, in Luke 18:35-41, we hear the story of the blind man who was sitting by the roadside begging. As Jesus was approaching Jericho, the beggar heard the crowd going by, and he asked what was happening. They told him that Jesus of Nazareth was passing by. The blind beggar called out, "Jesus, Son of David, have mercy on me!" Those who led the way rebuked him and told him to be quiet, but he shouted even more, "Son of David, have mercy on me." Jesus stopped and ordered the man to be brought to him. When he came near, Jesus asked him, "What do you want me to do for you?" He replied, "Lord, I want to see." Jesus said to him, "Receive your sight; your faith has healed you." Immediately, he received his sight and followed Jesus, praising God. When all the people saw it, they also praised God. Why did he use saliva and mud in the former case and use a simple word in the latter? He does whatever he wishes -- his ways are not our ways – but, ultimately, he wants to heal us for he came that we may have life and have it more abundantly (John 10:10).

In my ministry as a priest, I have witnessed Jesus heal people using sacramentals and using just a simple prayer. One of the instances when I witnessed healing using a sacramental was when I was working at Our Lady of Chiquiquira parish in Barranquilla, Colombia. A lady came and invited me to go and anoint her dad, who had had open-heart surgery. On the way, she said to me, "Father, I have a sister who is a Pentecostal. She often argues with me and criticizes the Catholic church, saying that we worship idols and pray to Mary and that we Catholics are all going to hell. I am sure she will be with my dad, so please, may I ask you a favour, do not argue with her if she begins her criticism." I told her not to worry because some of my siblings and relatives are non-

Catholics, and some are even members of Jehovah's Witnesses. I could understand what she was talking about; I was used to hearing those arguments.

When we got to their house, her sister was there with her dad. I prayed for their dad and anointed him with the Oil of the Sick. At the end of the prayers, I sprinkled Holy Water on everyone in the house, including her sister. I was waiting for her to ask why I used Holy Water, but she didn't; instead, she thanked me for coming to pray for her dad. She also said, "I felt the presence of the Holy Spirit here when you were praying." The following day, I offered a Mass of Healing at the parish. The church was packed with people and suddenly, a few minutes before the Mass started, a lady came to me. I recognized her as the Pentecostal lady whose father I had visited the day before. She asked to share a testimony with me. I thought it was about her father, whom I had anointed and asked what happened to him, but she said it was about her. I said, "Okay, tell me." She said that, as a Pentecostal, she never believed in the efficacy of the sacramentals or symbols we use for prayers as Catholics. She said she was losing her sight and could no longer read her Bible, which she treasured. I didn't know that she had a problem. When I was praying for her dad and all the sick, she said she was praying in her heart and asking God to heal her and restore her sight so that she could read the Word of God. After I prayed and started sprinkling the Holy Water, she said that a drop of the Water fell into her eyes, and instantly she recovered her sight. She said she saw and read clearly as if she had never had any eye problems. She said, "Now I believe that the Holy Water is powerful, and God can use anything to heal." I asked her if she was willing to share her testimony at the Healing Mass before I gave my homily, and she agreed. She stayed for the Healing Mass and gave her testimony to show her gratitude to God and to give Him glory and praise. Her sister couldn't believe what she saw, and she later told me that was the end of arguments and criticisms in their house against Catholics. God is good, and he works in mysterious ways.

Healing of incurable disease

After being tempted in the wilderness for forty days and forty nights and after defeating the devil, Jesus started his public ministry with this manifesto, "The Spirit of the Lord is upon me for he has anointed me to bring the good news to the poor. He has sent me to proclaim freedom for prisoners and recovery of sight for the blind, set the oppressed free, and proclaim the year of the Lord's favour" (Luke 4:18-19). Jesus went about doing good and curing all kinds of diseases -- even incurable ones. An example is a woman who had suffered from hemorrhages for more than thirty-eight years. She had spent all she had relying on the doctors but, instead of getting better, she was feeling worse. When she heard about Jesus and his healing power, she said, "If only I can touch the hem of his garment, I will be made well" (Mt. 9:21). The woman defied all odds and went through the crowd and touched his cloak; she was instantly made well. Jesus said, "Who touched me? For power has gone out of my body." She knelt, trembling, before Jesus. He said to her, "Woman, go in peace; your faith has saved you." It is amazing to see how Jesus can make the impossible possible when we put our faith and trust in him. When all hope is lost and human beings fail us, Jesus comes to restore our hope and life.

I witnessed such miraculous healing of a helpless and hopeless woman when I was working at Our Lady of Mount Carmel Parish, Espriella, in the diocese of Tumaco in Colombia. This parish was a missionary parish. We were three priests serving about forty-two communities. Some of the communities attended Mass only a few times a year, especially during Easter, Christmas, New Year or when there was a funeral or Memorial Mass in honour of a loved one who had died. Although the people are very religious, the lack of frequent Masses and proper catechesis affected their understanding and participation in the Holy Mass. Sometimes they didn't want to go to Mass unless it was a funeral or Memorial Mass. One Sunday morning, I was not scheduled for Mass and, since I preferred not to celebrate Mass alone, I decided to drive to one of the communities to celebrate with the people. When I got there, I invited the people but they told me, "Father, we did not know you were coming, and we are not ready for Mass today." I left them and went to another community about thirty minutes away. I invited them to Mass, and they said that their community had a soccer competition with another community and they were getting ready for the match. I left and drove to another community. By this time, it was almost noon. I invited the people to Mass, but they said it was already late; it was time to prepare lunch.

I was about to leave when the local catechist requested that I celebrate Mass with her and her sick dad. This community had no church. Masses were celebrated in the school. I asked the catechist to sweep one of the classes and get the place ready for Mass while I invited people to come from house to house. Some of the people I invited came, but the majority declined. I came to one house and saw a woman lying down in pain, crying. I asked her what the problem was. Like the woman from the Bible who suffered from hemorrhages, she said she had been sick for many years and had gone to many doctors. She had spent all she had but they told her that there was nothing else they could do for her medically-that she had to bear the pain. I didn't know what to do, so I invited her to come to Mass and tell Jesus her problem, that Jesus is the healer of the sick. I just said that to give her hope. I didn't even think she had the strength to come to Mass. Other people also complained of one ailment or another.

After Consecration, during the Mass, I told the people, "Here is Jesus, really present to us in his humanity and divinity. Some of you told me that you are sick or in pain. He is the one who heals and said he came that we may have life in abundance. Tell him what you want him to do for you; ask him to give you healing where it is needed most." I held the Blessed Sacrament elevated for about a minute so that they could speak to the Eucharistic Jesus. After that, I continued the Mass as usual. At the end of the Mass, I gave them a blessing and laid my hands on the sick among them and then left.

About six months later, I went to a Memorial Mass in another community and, before I started the Mass, a woman came and greeted me and hugged me very tightly. She asked, "Father, do you remember me?" I replied, "Have we met before?" She said, "Do you remember when you came to Mass in Albania and invited people to Mass from house to house?" I had almost forgotten, so I asked what had happened. She continued, "Do you remember the woman who told you that she was in great pain and had gone to many doctors and was told, "There is nothing else we can do for you." She said, "That day, I was dying, but when you said I should come to tell Jesus my problem, I felt that was my last hope. So, I asked some people to help take me to the church. After the Consecration, when you elevated the Host and asked us to tell Jesus to heal us, I said to him, "Lord Jesus, you know how much I have suffered and I am dying in pain. Please take away this pain from me, for there is nothing else the doctors can do for me. You are my last hope." She said that she immediately felt relief in her body. She was healed completely, and since that day, she has never experienced the pains again. She was so happy and grateful to God, and she said, "Now I know that Jesus Christ is present in the Eucharist." I asked her if she was ready to share this testimony at Mass and she said, "Yes." During the homily, I invited her to share her experience. She said, "My people, most of you know me and how much I have suffered severe pain due to my illness. Six months ago, when Father came to celebrate in our community, though I was in great pain, I attended the Mass specifically to pray for healing. I stand here to testify that I was completely healed at that Mass, free from pain. I now believe in the Real Presence, and I will never miss Mass again. Under normal circumstances, this woman would be the last person to stand up and speak in public, but that day she spoke so eloquently and powerfully that, in the end, she received a standing ovation from the crowd. Her testimony brought a change and transformation to that community. From that day on, I no longer had to go from house to house to invite people to Mass; instead, the people were readily waiting for me, and they participated actively during Mass. To God be all the glory! Whenever you're sick or have a sick loved one, I encourage you to bring your trouble to the Lord in prayer. If you can attend Mass or Adoration, go there and tell Jesus what you need him to do for you. Have faith and trust in his healing love and mercy. No sickness is beyond his power. He is the same yesterday, today and forever. He healed in the past, and he continues to heal today, so do not be afraid to approach him to ask for help.

Jesus still delivers and liberates

Part of Jesus' ministry was to liberate people from any forces that kept them in bondage. He healed people physically and spiritually by delivering those who were tormented by demons or evil spirits. As we read in Mk. 1:23-28, "Just then a man in their synagogue possessed by an impure spirit cried out, "What do you want with us, Jesus of Nazareth? Have you come to destroy us? I know who you are - the Holy One of God!" "Be quiet!" said Jesus sternly. "Come out of him!" The impure spirit shook the man violently and came out of him with a shriek. The people were all very amazed, and they asked each other, "What is this? A new teacher and with authority! He even gives orders to impure spirits, and they obey him." News about him spread quickly over the whole region of Galilee. Jesus also said in Lk 4:18 that he was anointed and sent to set the oppressed free. He didn't want the good news to stop with him, so he sent his apostles to continue that ministry of healing, deliverance and liberation. He also gave that power to heal, not just to the apostles or the ordained, but to all who believed in him.

As I said earlier, the reality of demonic attacks or possession seems not to be well known in the Western world, probably because of the advancement of science and technology. Sometimes, when someone has manifestations of spiritual attacks, these are confused with psychological or emotional problems. And most people, even ordained ministers, do not know how to discern the difference because they were never taught in their formation years or have never experienced it. I have had several experiences like that in the past. One day, I went to a Pentecost celebration in Medellin, Colombia, with Fr. John Mario Montoya, a very popular charismatic priest and a great preacher. We were in a stadium where about thirty thousand people were gathered. As praise and worship were going on, and Fr. John Mario was invoking the Holy Spirit, there were manifestations in the whole arena. Some people began to speak in tongues, and some began to experience demonic attacks. As they fell to the ground, the ushers carried them to a room where prayer warriors prayed for them. There was one woman who the devil tormented, and she was very aggressive. The prayer warriors tried to calm her down but had no success. So, they decided to look for a priest. There were more than sixty priests in the arena, and each of the priests they approached said that they didn't have any experience ministering to people experiencing such attacks.

I didn't have much experience either but, since no priest wanted to go, I decided to… not because I am holy or prayerful. I just felt that, as priests, Jesus has given us the power and authority to heal and expel demons; I relied on the promises of Jesus, not on my power. When I got to the room, as soon as the woman saw me, she looked directly into my eyes and shouted, "Get out from here, you black devil. What do you want from me? You are very ugly." That was precisely the type of thing the demoniac said to Jesus. The difference is that, in the case of Jesus, the demoniac recognized him as the Son of God who had the power to destroy him. But, in my case, the devil knew I was a sinner, and I was weak, so he spoke through the woman to put fear in me.

As you know, fear is one of the enemy's strategies against us. I replied to her, saying, "I know that I am ugly and unworthy, but from now on, you will no longer see my ugly face; you will see the beautiful face of Jesus." As soon as I said that, she closed her eyes and did not open them again until we had finished our prayers. Friends, there is power in the name of Jesus. Any time the devil accuses you of your sins, call on the name of Jesus and claim your authority in his name. It was a challenging situation, and we had a long prayer of deliverance. The more we prayed, the more the spirits in her resisted. They were speaking through her saying, "We are legion, this is our abode, we are not leaving, we have come to destroy her." I rebuked them each time they spoke and claimed deliverance and liberation for her in the mighty Name of Jesus and by the Precious Blood of Jesus. In the end, to the glory of God, she was delivered.

When she opened her eyes, she said, "I am seeing a light, the light of Christ." She began to sing a song of praise to God for saving her life and setting her free. She gave me a big hug and said, "You are the most beautiful person I have ever seen in my life." When she was in bondage and darkness, she could not see anything good in me. She called me "black devil and ugly," but when she was liberated and entered the kingdom of light, she saw the image of God; she saw the beautiful face of Jesus in me.

There is always a transformation when we experience the healing and merciful love of Jesus. The old order gives way to the new order, we become new creatures in Christ Jesus, and we see reality differently. That was the type of transformation St. Paul had when he went to Damascus to persecute Christians. He was blind until he encountered Jesus on the way. Jesus asked him, "Saul, Saul, why are you persecuting me?" Saul replied, "Who are you?" and Jesus replied, "I am Jesus whom you are persecuting" (Acts 9:4-5). When his eyes opened, instead of seeing Christians as enemies, he began to see them as brothers and sisters; his life changed, and so did his name – from Saul to Paul. I have witnessed many other miracles during my ministry. Most of them follow the same pattern but, in the end, God has always been faithful to his words and promises. There is a significant change that can be noticed in the life of the victims. They feel free, liberated, joyful, and grateful, and often they sing praises to God.

Some of the things I learned from praying for people under demonic attacks are:

1) Never become afraid of the devil because, as St. John says, "He who is in you is greater than he who is in the world" (1 John 1:4-5).

2) Never rely on your own power or holiness; always rely on the power of the Holy Spirit and call on the Name of Jesus. The Holy Spirit knows and understands all truths and the enemy's tricks. The name of Jesus is so powerful that the enemy cannot resist him. Cover yourself with the Precious Blood of Jesus and cover your family and everyone praying with you.

3) Be humble and acknowledge your sinfulness and ask for God's mercy and forgiveness so that the enemy has no ground to accuse you. If you can go to confession before embarking on deliverance prayer, that will be great. But if you don't have the opportunity, make an Act of Contrition and give your sins to Jesus and, like the tax collector in Luke 18:13, tell him, "Lord, be merciful to me a sinner."

4) Claim your authority from the Word of God and rely entirely on the help of God, our Lord Jesus, the angels and the saints. Our Blessed Mother Mary and Archangel Michael have always been my great intercessors during deliverance prayers. God is faithful to his Word, and he never fails those who put their trust in him, so do not be afraid.

It is not about my sins but about God's mercy

A prayer group in Barranquilla, Colombia, had invited me for a talk one weekend. It was a beautiful day, and the prayer conference took place in a resort near a beach. There were about seventy to eighty people in attendance. I was dressed in my African attire, so many people who didn't know me before didn't recognize me as a priest. When I arrived at the resort, they were already in the middle of a praise and worship and prayer session. I quietly entered and took my place. After the praise and worship, I was invited to give the talk.

I was aware of my human limitations, sinfulness and brokenness, and I hadn't had the opportunity to attend Confession. While the prayer was going on, I could not concentrate; I was filled with a sense of guilt, and my conscience was heavy. The enemy took advantage of that and accused me, "You are unworthy. How can you preach the Word of God when you are a sinner? You are a hypocrite; God will not listen to you… Shame on you…." All these words played in my mind, and I was so confused and restless that I couldn't coordinate my ideas.

I could only think about my past sins and how unworthy I was. Suddenly, it was time for me to speak and I was introduced and invited to take the stage. Within me, I was so ashamed of myself; I felt powerless.

Of course, the people didn't know what was going on in my mind. I knelt and asked the people to pray over me before I gave my talk. As they prayed over me, the Holy Spirit inspired me to rebuke the enemy's negative and condemnatory thoughts. I prayed silently, "Lord, I am sorry for my sins. Please forgive me and be merciful to me and wash away my sins with the Precious Blood of Jesus. Devil, get behind me; I did not sin against you. I sinned against God, and he is a merciful and forgiving God. He sent Jesus to come and die for my sins even before I came into being. He has paid the price for my sins with his death on the cross, so do not accuse me again because I have been forgiven." As soon as I finished that prayer, it seemed like magic. All the guilt and heaviness in my heart and conscience were lifted. I felt instant relief and joy.

When I began to preach, the words flowed; the Holy Spirit took over, and there was much anointing in the place. At the end of the preaching, I invited the band to sing some praise and worship music while I ministered to the people in prayer. The prayer and anointing were so powerful that everyone in the arena was filled with the Holy Spirit, and they rested in the Spirit. It was the most powerful ministration I have experienced in my ministry as a priest. It was amazing, and everyone felt the glory of God.

Now, there was a security man at the gate of the resort. He was not part of the group but observed what was happening from the gate. When he saw about eighty people on the floor, he said, "From where did they get this African abracadabra man?" He thought, "I will see if this is real or if they are pretending. This man will not push me down; I will make sure I resist it." I didn't know what was going on in his mind, so I closed my eyes and placed my hands on him when he came to me for prayer. He wanted to fall, but I noticed he resisted. I continued to pray for him, and he staggered, still resisting. Then I said, "Whatever spirit of resistance in him, I command you to leave in the name of Jesus Christ." Immediately, he fell to the floor. Because he was the last person to be prayed over, he was lying down there for about thirty minutes. We concluded the event, and almost everyone had left before he woke up. When he woke up, he gave me a big hug and asked me, "What must I do?" Without knowing what had happened to him, I asked him, "What do you mean by 'what must I do'?" It was then that he began to give testimony of what had happened to him while he was on the floor.

He said, "Father, I want to confess that I am a sinner." He told me all his sins and said, "From today, I will never sin again; I will give my life to Jesus. Please tell me what to do." He continued, "When I saw you enter, I didn't know you were a priest. When you started praying for people, and they were falling, I thought, 'From where did they bring this African abracadabra man.' I came to see what you would do, telling myself, 'This man will not push me down.' When you prayed for me and placed your hand on me, it felt like an electric current going through my body; I felt warm. I wanted to fall, but I resisted. When you placed your hand on my forehead, it seemed like a weight was laid upon me. I staggered but thought, 'I will not fall for this man.' Then, when you commanded whatever spirit of resistance was in me to leave in the name of Jesus, it seemed that the whole world's weight was laid on me, and I couldn't resist anymore; then I fell. I was transported to the spiritual world when I was on the ground. I heard the angels and saints praising God, and I heard Jesus saying that he loves me unconditionally, that it was because of me that he died on the cross and wants me to experience peace and joy for all eternity. The more the voice spoke, the more I felt at peace and happy, such that I wanted to remain there forever without coming back to this world. That was why I didn't want to wake up until you woke me up. Father, please tell me what I need to do; I will change my way of living. I don't want anything to prevent me from experiencing this peace and joy forever."

That day, I realized that it was not about me but about Jesus and whatever he wanted to do with me and through me. That day, I realized that "In persona Christi" means "In the person of Christ." As priests, we serve in the person of Christ. God chose us not because we are holy but because of his love and mercy. He chose us not because we are strong or perfect; instead, he chose the weak and the imperfect so that when he uses us to accomplish his work, we don't think it is because we are holy or intelligent or powerful. We give him all the glory because we know that healing occurs only by his grace and power; it is not about us. That day the Word of God in Hebrews became more apparent to me.

> "Every high priest is chosen from among the people and is appointed to represent the people in matters related to God, to offer gifts and sacrifices for sins. He can deal gently with those who are ignorant and go astray since he is subject to weakness. This is why he has to offer sacrifices for his sins and the sins of the people. And no one takes this honour on himself, but he receives it when called by God, just as Aaron was. In the same way, Christ did not take on himself the glory of becoming a high priest. But God said to him, "You are my Son; today I have become your Father" (Hebrews 5:1-6).

As priests and Christians, we are called to live a holy life and lead by example. But the fact remains that we, though priests, are all broken and wounded; yet we are called to care for those who are broken and wounded because we can identify with them. If we were not broken and wounded, we might become judgmental, unloving, and unmerciful. Jesus wants us to reflect the Father's merciful love in the world through the sacraments – not because we are worthy but because he is worthy. Only our Lord and Saviour, Jesus Christ, is the holy and perfect one. Therefore, we must always focus on him as our model, not on any priest or leader of the Church. If our faith is built on Jesus, the rock and firm foundation, we will be able to withstand whatever storm we face in life.

Miracle of conversion in one hour

In 2017, I was invited by a prayer group in Barranquilla, Colombia to give a talk at a conference. When I landed in the capital, Bogota, I took a local flight to Barranquilla. Sitting beside me was a stranger who became a great friend by the time we landed. It all started with a phone call from the organizers of the conference, wondering when our flight was leaving. At the end of the conversation, the man sitting beside me asked, "Where are you from?" I replied, "I am a Nigerian, but I live in Canada." He said, "I noticed when you were speaking that you have a different accent, and I was curious to know where you come from, and what you are doing in Colombia." I replied that I am a priest and here for a conference. He asked me, "Are you really a Catholic priest?" I said, "Yes, and what about you?" He replied, "I am also a Catholic, but I don't practice my faith. I go to church about twice a year or at times when my wife invites me." "Why don't you practice your faith?" I enquired. He said, "I am an engineer and have many projects around the country, so I am swamped during the week, visiting our sites and supervising our projects. Sunday is usually the only day I get the opportunity to rest so, to be honest, I don't feel the need to go to church."

This response led to a very interesting conversation that lasted through the flight. I asked him such soul-searching questions as – "Why are you here on earth, or what is your purpose in life? Who makes it possible for you to have all these contracts and success in your career? Is it because of your smartness or great connections?

Don't you see it as a sign of God's love and blessings? How are you showing gratitude for all your blessings? Do you know that some people have boarded a flight or embarked on a journey and never reached their destination? What if this is your last flight and day here on earth? What would happen to all those projects, your money in the bank, and those that prevent you from having a relationship with God? What would you tell God when you come to Him? Do you believe that our meeting today, travelling on the same flight, sitting in the same row, and having this conversation just happened by chance? I think it's a way of God calling your attention and inviting you to reflect on your life, priorities, and choices."

He affirmed what I said, was open and honest in answering the questions and discussing his struggles. The Holy Spirit was powerfully present during our conversation, and he testified that his heart was touched and burning as I shared the Word of God with him. Before we reached our destination, right there on the plane, he requested to go to Confession and committed to change his ways and go back to church. He was filled with so much peace and joy. That was a miracle! He asked me about the conference that I was going to speak at, promising to attend. As soon as we landed, deplaned and claimed our luggage, he called his wife who came to pick him up. He said to her, "Come, I want to introduce someone special I just met on the plane. What you couldn't achieve in fifteen years, God has used this man to achieve in one hour. God has answered the prayers you have been praying for me since we married. The husband who left you a week ago is not the same man coming back to you today. I am now a new person." He was vibrating with joy and smiles as he was saying all this. He told his wife about the conference and collected the information about the venue and where I was staying during my visit.

The following morning, before 8 a.m., he came with his wife and children to where I was staying. His wife said, "Father, I can't believe what I see. I have been praying for the conversion of my husband for the past fifteen years. I was on the verge of giving up hope. This is truly a miracle, and I thank God for bringing you into his life." She continued, "For the first time in fifteen years, I have seen my husband truly happy; we prayed together last night and this morning. He couldn't stop talking about his experience on the plane and how his heart was burning with joy. You shared the word of God with him, just like the two disciples experienced on the road to Emmaus when Jesus appeared to them after the resurrection and explained the scriptures (Luke 24:13-35). We are here this morning as a family to thank God for what he did in the life of my husband/family through you in just one hour." It was a fantastic experience that brought me close to the family – we became good friends. To show his gratitude, the man cancelled all his appointments and business trips for one week, attended the conference with his wife, and drove me to Cartagena to visit some of my friends. By the time I left, my friend and his wife promised to get married in the church when next I visited Barranquilla. As God would have it, I visited again in 2019, and I presided at their wedding. They said their marriage, relationship and family life had been blessed. They now participate in a Couples Prayer Group in their church. They have participated in couples retreats and other events that help them grow in their faith, communication, and relationship as a couple. They have experienced some difficult moments, but having God in their life, through prayer and sharing the Word of God, they have been able to support each other in good times and in bad.

This experience speaks to the power of prayer and the need to share the word of God with others, even strangers we meet while travelling. It also shows that with God, nothing is impossible. He can use you as an instrument to touch hearts if you are open to following the promptings of the Holy Spirit. Anywhere can be a place for an encounter with Jesus and the living God, and he always has time for everyone. Therefore, keep your hope alive, trust the Lord, and bring him all your needs.

Suggested Action: Please take a moment and say a little prayer for those struggling in their faith, for priests, missionaries, evangelists, and church leaders; that they may have the courage to share the good news with love and passion. Pray for their protection as they are targets of the enemy because he knows that he has succeeded in destroying many souls if he gets one priest or leader.

Prayer: Dear Jesus, thank you for the gift of our priests. Please heal their brokenness and protect them from the evil one. May they rely completely on your love, mercy and power and not on their own power as they minister to your people. Through them, may many souls be drawn closer to you, and continue to use them as your instrument of healing. Amen!

9

Mission to Canada: a source of many blessings

Towards the end of my mission in Colombia, my friend Jenny came to me and said she saw me in a dream, going on a mission to Canada. I didn't pay much attention to what she said because I had a different plan. My superior had invited me to work at the seminary (The Claretian Institute of Philosophy, Nekede, Owerri, Nigeria) as the Dean of Students. I happily accepted because it is my Alma Mater and because I love the seminarians and wanted to share my missionary experience with them, believing it would help encourage them in their vocational journey. I must confess that I had a wonderful experience with the students. We established a beautiful friendship and relationship that has lasted until today.

During my stay in the seminary, I had some uncomfortable disagreements with the then superior regarding his administrative style and approach to the formation of our seminarians. Instead of quarrelling with him, I requested to leave for another mission but it was denied. Coincidentally, I was chatting with one of my friends, a former Claretian, who left to join a diocese in Canada. He told me that there was a great need for priests in the Archdiocese of Halifax. I asked him to inquire if the bishop would be interested in having me work there. As a result, I was invited to go to Halifax for a vacation in 2007 to meet with the bishop. Unfortunately, by the time I arrived, that bishop had been transferred. I met with an administrator who told me that he could not make any decision since he was not a bishop. He asked me to come back for a visit in 2008 to meet with Archbishop Mancini, which I did. After going through a period of prayerful discernment and due process, he welcomed me to the Archdiocese in 2009.

Leaving the Claretian Order and my country was tough and painful for me because I had a great relationship with most of the Claretian order members and my friends and family in Nigeria. I felt sad and knew that I would miss them all, but it was the right decision at that time. Today, looking back at all the amazing experiences that have happened in my life and ministry here in Canada, I can see God's hand in everything – even in the disagreement I had with my superior and other circumstances beyond my control which changed my plan, leading to my coming to Canada. My friend's dream eventually became a reality. God's plan is always the best, but we tend to worry because we are so limited in our perception of realities. The Lord continually reminds us to trust in him and not be afraid, especially in our darkest moments. My coming to Canada has been a great source of blessing in many ways, and I pray it will continue to be for the glory of God and for the good of all the people I serve. God has been faithful to his Word and has used my ministry to bring his people healing, life, and hope.

Healing as a Christmas gift

"Whatever you ask in my name, I will do it" (John 14:13).

When I was the pastor of St. Genevieve's parish in East Chezzetcook, Nova Scotia, one of my parishioners invited me to visit her mother at the hospital. She was supposed to have heart surgery the following day. I went and prayed with her mom and anointed her. The next day, before she was taken to the operating theatre, the doctors wanted to run another test to ensure her condition remained the same as their tests had shown. To their great surprise, they could no longer see the blockage. They did another scan, and everything was clear. They were astounded. They told her they could no longer find anything wrong with her heart, and she was discharged. This happened a few days before Christmas. My parishioner was so thrilled that she called the healing of her mom's heart disease her Christmas gift. There is nothing impossible to God.

Witnesses of healing

The fact that Jesus heals and wants us to pray for healing is an experience many people have witnessed. At my parish, Christ the King in Dartmouth, as part of our Pentecost challenge or update on our Stewardship of Treasure Booklet, we encourage parishioners to share their witness of the miracles God is bringing about in their lives. We have received an abundance of witnesses and testimonies of the transformation people are experiencing in their lives, including miraculous healings. I would like to share one such witnessing to show there is power in intercessory prayers – asking other people to pray for us. And I encourage you to pray for physical healing because our Lord Jesus still heals, and he says, "Whatever you ask in my name, I will do it" (John 14:13). A parishioner of mine shares with us a healing experience he had, as he recounts:

"Friday, March 12, 2021, started as a typical Friday until just after lunch. While running errands, I developed intense pain in my jaw. Realizing that this was not normal and potentially serious, I drove directly to Emergency at the Dartmouth General Hospital. I was quickly assessed, and it was determined that I was experiencing a heart attack. I was put on a stretcher, and within seconds my clothes were removed and six people started attending to me. I was given medication, monitored, and then transferred by ambulance to the QEII Cardiac Cath Lab. At the lab, they tried to install a stent to bypass a plaque blockage but were unsuccessful. I remained in the ICU. Sunday, they attempted the stent procedure a second time, which was also unsuccessful. Due to bed shortages, I was transported back to ICU at Dartmouth General Hospital Monday evening under the care of a cardiologist.

That week, I continued having an evolving heart attack which had to run its course. I was closely monitored and medicated as my blood pressure did not go higher than thirty-five. Thursday morning, the Cardiologist said that, since I wasn't improving, the only option was a pacemaker, and he had scheduled the procedure for Friday at the QEII. My wife went home and called our family and friends across Canada and her prayer groups to pray that if I needed to have this procedure, so be it, and let it be done safely to help improve my situation. During the night, I woke to feel something change in my body. I didn't know what it was, but I just felt different. The following day the cardiologist came into my room and informed me that my heart rate and the electrical firing in my heart had returned to normal. He was amazed and couldn't explain what had happened, but I no longer needed the pacemaker and surgery was cancelled. By the grace of God, I was almost back to normal. I stayed in the hospital until Monday so that they could monitor my walking around with no issues. I know that a higher power (God) was at work to help me through this heart attack. The hospital visit with Father T, the hundreds of prayers, and the care provided by the hospital and ambulance staff all accounted for my miracle. I do not take this lightly and am enjoying life with family and friends. Thanks!" (Ken Rankin).

Some others have expressed experiencing emotional, psychological and spiritual healing after prayers and counselling sessions. I will gather those testimonies and share them with the permission of the individuals concerned to give glory and praise to God.

Suggested Action: Visit someone sick at the hospital, at home or in a nursing home. Pray for their physical, emotional, psychological and spiritual healing.

Prayer: Lord Jesus, fill me with your love and make me an instrument of your healing love and mercy for your people. Amen!

10

Mission accomplished at death

"For none of us live for ourselves alone, and none of us dies for ourselves alone. If we live, we live for the Lord; and if we die, we die for the Lord. So, whether we live or die, we belong to the Lord. For this reason, Christ died and returned to life so that he might be the Lord of both the dead and the living" (Romans 14:7-9).

I strongly believe in the above scriptural passage and believe that everyone born into this world has a mission. Sometimes one may not realize their mission until they die and return to God. Many experiences have shown me that God can accomplish his purpose through us, even at our death. I will share two occasions where the dead fulfilled a mission without physically being there and without knowing that could be one of the reasons why God brought them into this world.

God used someone's death to bring life to others

One experience of a death fulfilling a mission happened in 2008 when I visited Halifax for the second time while discerning whether to join the Archdiocese. I was assigned to the then Blessed Mother Theresa of Calcutta parish in North End Halifax for six weeks. The pastor, Fr. Gilbert, OMI, could not be there for the wake, and he asked me to go. Since I did not have my car, the secretary, Mary, called one of the parishioners, Josie

Ritcey, to drive me to the wake. When we arrived at the funeral home, we were told it was scheduled for the following day. So, we had to go back and laughed over it. On our way to the parish, I began a conversation with

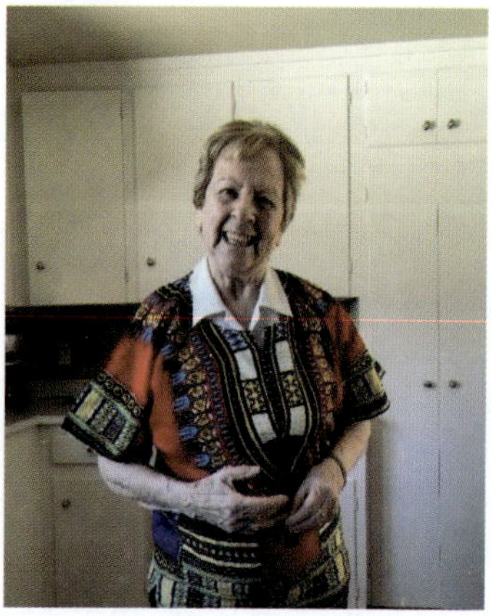

Josie Ritcey – a woman with a heart of gold

Josie. She was very pleasant and friendly, and she wanted to know everything about my country, Nigeria, and my family. She also told me about her family and Cape Breton where she was born and raised. We got to know each other's family backgrounds in that short period as if we had known each other for ages. That was the beginning of a very good and beautiful friendship that has lasted until now.

The following day, Josie drove me to the wake and afterwards, we continued to talk over the phone even when I went back to Nigeria to continue the discernment process. Through getting to know me, Josie has gotten to know my family and many people in my hometown, and she has sponsored many children in school. These children would not have been able to receive an education and help without me getting to know Josie. And perhaps I would not have gotten to know Josie if that man had not died when I was at Blessed Mother

Theresa parish. Though the man's death caused pain and grief to his family, God used his death to give life to others. So, I believe part of his mission on earth was to bring Josie and me together – but he didn't know that. I guess he might have wondered when he was alive what his mission in life was. He may have even felt that he hadn't accomplished anything. But God works in mysterious ways. He has a purpose for bringing us into this world, and whether we are alive or dead, God's purpose in our lives will be fulfilled.

Suicide that became a saving grace for a family

Another experience of someone fulfilling a mission at the time of death happened in 2014 when I was at St. Mary's Basilica in Halifax. At St. Patrick's Church, I celebrated the funeral of a twenty-five-year-old man who died of suicide. He was a lovely and friendly young man, very popular in the community. The church was packed full of people on the funeral day, especially young people. Everyone was crying and feeling devastated. Such a funeral is a hard one to celebrate and preach at. Based on the Word of God, I tried to give words of consolation to the family and friends who were grieving and mourning. Also, I encouraged all those present to learn from the young man's death to make peace with God and their family and not procrastinate because we do not know what could happen tomorrow.

A few weeks later, I was appointed pastor of St. Genevieve Parish, East Chezzetcook, Nova Scotia. After a few months, I went to the Pastoral Center in Halifax to get some documents signed. While I was in the parking lot, a woman came and gave me a big hug with a smile of gratitude. I asked if she was a parishioner at the Basilica, but she was not. She said, "Father, you do not know me, but I was present at the funeral of the young man who died by suicide which you celebrated at St. Patrick's Church some time ago." She continued, "Before that funeral, I was having a crisis of faith; I had stopped going to church because of the scandals in the Church.

To make matters worse, I was having many problems with my husband, to the point that we had decided to divorce. We had gone to the lawyer to fill out the forms and were supposed to go on Monday to sign the documents. The funeral was on Friday. My heart was broken when I went to that funeral Mass, but what you said during the homily touched my heart, and I left the church a changed person. When I got home, I spoke with my husband, and we decided to work on our relationship. And I went back to Church. Since then, I feel so happy to be back to my faith, and my marriage has been saved. I know it was an unfortunate and painful experience for his family, but I want to tell you that what you said at the funeral of that young man was a saving grace for me. His mission was to save my soul and my family." That was amazing! I am sure that the young man's parents did not know what happened at their son's funeral. They did not know that God used his tragic death and their pain to save a life and a marriage. God works in mysterious ways. No wonder St. Paul says, "We know that everything works unto good to those who love God" (Romans 8:20). So, in life and death, we belong to God.

Suggested action: Pray for a loved one who has died and the souls in purgatory.

Prayer: Dear God, grant eternal rest to all our loved ones and comfort those still grieving and mourning their loss. Give them your peace and strength and help them know that the one they loved has accomplished their mission even if they can't see it now. We pray in Jesus' name. Amen!

11

The birth of Boniface and Paulina Okafor Memorial Hospital and the Family Care Program

"And you know that God anointed Jesus of Nazareth with the Holy Spirit and with power. Then Jesus went about doing good (feeding the hungry, curing the sick) and healing all who were oppressed by the devil, for God was with him" (Acts 10:38).

As we see in different passages of scripture, the attitude of Jesus towards those who were suffering – the sick, the poor and sinners – was always an attitude of love, compassion and care. He not only healed the sick, he also gave food to the hungry. The mission he gave his disciples was not just a mission to heal but also a mission to feed the hungry and teach and provide care for the poor and needy. As I said earlier, growing up after the civil war was a very tough experience. I know what it means to suffer and go without food or life necessities. I believe that is what made me more sensitive to the plight of the poor and needy, coupled with the examples of my parents and my first parish priest, Fr. Kevin Ikpa. I have always had the desire to make people's lives better. That is one of the reasons that I was motivated to embrace the priestly life. By the grace of God, I try my humble best to support those I can with the help of my friends and benefactors who generously support me in my ministry.

Two incidents led to the establishment of the charitable organization known as BAPOM Hospital and Family Care Program. The first happened in 2012 when one of my brothers-in-law was attacked with a bucket of acid by an enemy for no apparent reason. There was no hospital in our area where he could be treated. The nearest hospital was Umunze, about a forty-minute drive from our home. Before they got there, the acid had burned the greater part of my brother-in-law's body. And to make matters worse, on reaching the hospital, they were told that the acid burn was too severe and they could not treat him. Since it was very dangerous to commute at night in Nigeria, he stayed at the hospital all night without treatment. You can imagine how terrible and painful the experience was for him and all the family.

The next day, when he got to a bigger hospital at UNTH Enugu, the staff there could not handle it well either, so we took him to another private hospital at Owerri and later to Orlu. He had six plastic surgeries to treat the burns but, unfortunately, these were unsuccessful. Then we decided to send him to India for treatment and surgery, which cost over 50,000 USD.

Thanks to the generosity of my parishioners and friends, we were able to raise some funds, and I took a loan to make up the difference. I thank God that my brother-in-law survived it, even though he is still suffering the effects of the wounds and has lost one of his eyes.

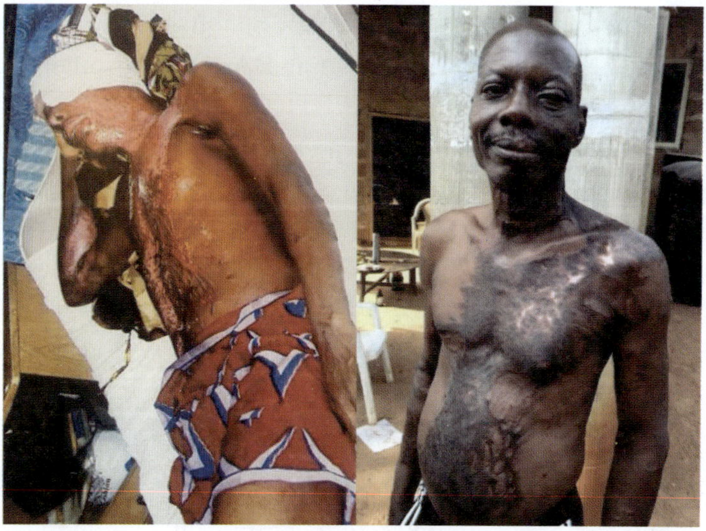

Pictures of my brother-in-law
before and after his surgery and recovery

The second event was when one of my uncles was going to have his blood pressure checked. He fell on the road and, because we had no nearby hospital, he died before they could get a car to take him to a hospital. I said to myself, "If we had a hospital in my village, perhaps my brother-in-law would not have suffered so much, and my uncle might have been saved had they taken him to the hospital in time." I also thought of all the people in my village who cannot afford to go to India or to other hospitals. I said to myself, "You can get mad or criticize the government for lack of healthcare and basic amenities, but that will not change anything; your people will continue to die. So, one gains nothing by cussing the darkness; what is needed is to light a candle to dispel it." That was when I thought, "I must build a hospital in my village to help my people, especially the poor and the needy who cannot afford to travel far for medical care, so that they will not suffer like my uncle and brother-in-law."

That dream to establish a hospital became a reality when I arrived at St. Thomas More Church in 2014. I met parishioners Anne and Deacon Jim McLevey. This was before the amalgamation of three parishes – St. Vincent de Paul, St. Thomas More and the French community, Mission La Sainte Famille – into one named Christ the King Parish. During one of our conversations, Anne and Jim told me that they spearhead a charitable organization through which they help low-income families in India. After I shared the experiences and difficult situation in my home community, they asked the Canada Revenue Agency if they could extend help to the poor in Nigeria using the same India Helper Program charitable status. The response was affirmative. Therefore, with the help of the coordinating team in Canada, we decided to start the Nigeria Family Helper Program on July 6, 2016.

Anne & Deacon Jim McLevey
Instruments of God's love

Sr. Dr. Joannes Uzoma – Instrument of God's love and healing

While I was discerning whether to embark on the hospital project or not, I prayed about it and spoke to some of my friends to hear their thoughts. The first person was Sr. Dr. Joannes Uzoma, who told me it was a good idea since there was no hospital in our community. She volunteered to help and was instrumental in registering the hospital with the Abia State Ministry of Health.

Another person was a friend of mine from Colombia, Dr. Alcira Alba, a woman with a heart filled with love for Jesus and Mary. She is a lay missionary, and we had done some missionary outreach together when I was in Colombia.

Dr. Alcira Alba and Fr. Toochukwu

Dr. Alcira with her husband Freddy, late mum Olivia and her sister Angela

After visiting Nigeria in 2006 for an international conference at Madonna University in Elele and seeing the poverty and great need of the people, she was willing to go for a six months (up to a year) mission in Nigeria to provide free medical service to the hospital. I would say that it was through her that God confirmed to me that I should move ahead with the hospital project. I say that because I was praying and said to God, "If it is your will that I should start a hospital, I need a sign – let someone send me some money for the business registration." At about noon that day, I received a call from Elizabeth Morrisey informing me that her daughter, Angela, who works for the Johnson & Johnson pharmaceutical company, would like to donate some medications for my people in Nigeria as I was going there for a vacation at that time. I wondered whether that was the answer to my prayer. I said to myself, "No," because I specifically asked God for money for the registration. The whole day had almost passed and I hadn't received any money, so I thought I would not continue with the project. To my great surprise, at about 11:30 pm, after I had shut down my computer and was getting ready to go to bed, I received a phone text message from Alcira. I opened the message and couldn't believe what I saw. She wrote: "I was praying for you today and thought about your dream to open a hospital in your village. I decided to send you a little money via Western Union to help toward the opening of the hospital project." I said, "Woah! What a miracle!" I jumped up and started praising God. When we had our team meeting the next day, I shared the experience with them, and they were all happy. However, we also needed some money to renovate my father's old house to make sure it met the standards of a clinic as stipulated by the Ministry of Health. Right then and there, Gary and Rosemary Moore generously donated the money for the renovation. I became convinced that God's hand was behind the project. He is the Divine Provider, and he has provided for us ever since we started through the generosity of men and women of goodwill.

The hospital and Family Care projects were founded to help needy people in the Eastern part of Nigeria. The hospital is located at Umudim Ngodo Isuochi, Umunneochi Local Government Area in Abia. It is a rural community with approximately thirty-thousand inhabitants. Sixty percent of the population is made up of children and youth. Most inhabitants of this village are farmers and petty traders who are not financially capable of caring for their basic needs. Unfortunately, there are no social amenities like steady electricity, water, good roads, a government hospital, etc., in the whole town.

The nearest good government hospitals are at Enugu, Umuahia, or Owerri, about eighty to eighty-five kilometres away. Under normal circumstances, it would be an hour and a half journey but, due to bad roads, sometimes it may take over two hours or more to get to the hospital.

The government does not provide any health insurance or basic amenities. Medical care and treatment are solely the patient's or their family's responsibility, and one must pay upfront for medical consultation and any drugs or treatment received. If a person doesn't have any money, they are left to suffer or face possible death unless God, in His infinite mercy, grants healing to the sick person. Because of this, most people who do not have money for their treatment pray and look to God for healing. This has led to the proliferation of spiritual healing centers, native or traditional healing shrines, or patent medicine stores. Those who run the spiritual healing ministries/centers often have no pastoral or theological formation. They take advantage of their patients' vulnerability. Also, most of those who manage patent medicine stores or prescribe and administer medications don't have any formal training. This has led to many health complications and deaths.

It is disheartening to see common tropical diseases like malaria killing many children, young people, and adults. Also, many people die of other minor illnesses that are preventable or curable. Due to a lack of proper health care and proximity to a hospital/health center, many young women have died during childbirth. Some young women have complications during delivery because there was no proper prenatal care. Some patients suffering from high blood pressure or diabetes cannot easily go to the hospital to control or monitor their conditions because they can't afford the transportation or cost of the tests. This sometimes has led to complications or even sudden death that otherwise could have been prevented or controlled.

Sadly, some of my family members and relatives died because of a lack of easy access to a hospital when they were sick. There are many children whose parents cannot send them to school or who have no house to live in. In the face of these dehumanizing situations and suffering, we felt the urge to do something to alleviate the suffering and pain of the poor in our community.

We aim to bring healthcare services (a hospital) closer to the people, provide free medical consultation and, in some cases, free medication/drugs. Where free medication is not possible, it will be given at a subsidized rate. We hope that with access to health care and proper psychoeducation, the health and living conditions of the beneficiaries will be improved significantly. Accessing a hospital and obtaining drugs from a certified doctor and genuine pharmaceutical companies will reduce the high risk of consuming adulterated drugs and the consequent side effects and health complications.

With the renovations finished, we successfully applied for the hospital registration, which has been a great blessing to our community and has saved many lives. More information about the hospital and its success stories will be included at the end of this book for anyone who would like to know more about it.

Suggested action: You can donate blood to your local blood bank and give food and clothing or financial support to the poor and needy around you. You can also serve in a soup kitchen, food bank, or daily bread homes.

Prayer: Lord Jesus, please bless and reward abundantly all those who give generously to support the poor and the needy. May we be sensitive to the needs of the poor so that through us, they may experience the love, mercy, and providence of our loving God. Amen!

12

God meets all my needs

"The Lord is my Shepherd; I shall not want" (Psalm 23-1).

It is amazing to see the fruits of God's goodness and mercy in this project! Through this experience and many others, I have come to understand the profound meaning of Psalm 23 and have equally understood the saying, "Givers never lack."

Once, a woman came to me asking for help; she had cancer and needed money for chemotherapy. At that time, I was still a member of the Claretian Order, living in Colombia. Because I was on my way to Venezuela to renew my passport (Nigeria had no embassy in Colombia at the time), I had just made a request of the bursar for money to buy shoes and other basic needs. This request had been granted, but when I saw the woman's condition and that she had two little children, I decided to give her the money. When I arrived in Venezuela, I attended Mass at one of the parishes belonging to the Claretian Missionaries. The pastor introduced me to the people and asked me to celebrate the Mass. He also told me that there were some Colombians in the parish. After Mass, a lady came to welcome me and said she was from Colombia. She invited me to dinner and offered me a tour around the city.

When we got to her apartment, her son, a professor at the university, offered to take me out so that he could give me a tour of their university. It was a beautiful city and the people were very friendly. At the end of the tour, he said he would like to give me a souvenir to remember my visit to Venezuela. When he asked me if I needed anything, I told him I needed some shoes. Coincidentally, there was a shoe shop on the other side of the street, so we went there. He asked me to pick any pair. The pair I liked was costly, so I was reluctant to tell him. He saw that I was looking at them and asked if I wanted them. I replied, "Yes, but they are very expensive." To put it in context, I was given sixty dollars for a pair of shoes and the one I saw cost $120.00. He told the saleslady to package two pairs of shoes for me – one black and one brown. I couldn't believe what I was hearing. He paid for both pairs of shoes and also gave me twice as much money as I had given to the woman with cancer. I was speechless, but in my heart, I said, "Woah, the Lord is truly my shepherd." We can never outdo God in generosity. When we give, we receive, as givers never lack!

A God of Divine Providence

One morning, I received a message that a brother-in-law was sick and that the family had no money for his treatment. When I called them to enquire how much they needed, they said seventy thousand Naira (₦70,000), which, at that time, was equivalent to about five hundred Canadian dollars (C$500). Since I didn't have that much money, I went to the chapel to pray. I thanked God for the gift of a new day and said other prayers. I prayed thus, "Dear Lord, you know about the message I received from home, and I don't have that amount of money. Please heal my brother-in-law and make it possible for me to help him." Later, I went to get ready to say Mass. As I entered the sacristy, I saw an envelope on the table with my name on it. I opened it and saw $500 in it, equivalent to the exact amount needed by my brother-in-law to go to the hospital. Immediately after Mass, I went to Western Union to send the money.

On my way, a friend of mine from Colombia called me. She is a single mother, and one of her sons was sick and needed about $200 to go to the hospital. I decided to send her the $200 right away, leaving me $200 short of the money I needed to send to my brother-in-law. While sending the money to my Colombian friend, I received a text message from another friend in the States, Sulima Rojas. I didn't look at the message until I got into my car. When I opened it, I read, "Father, I was thinking of you today and wanted to send you some money for your needs. You can go to Western Union to claim it." She had sent me $200, the exact amount I gave to my friend in Colombia. Our God never fails; he never disappoints.

He knows it all

In Nigeria, we sponsor many children to enable them to attend school. On one occasion, when a new school semester was about to start, I was called with a reminder of the tuition fees and other needs. I told them that I had no money at the time and that they should pray for Divine providence. I also went to my chapel to pray.

I told God, "Lord, you know these children need to go back to school, and I don't have the money. If you want them to continue their studies, please provide for me to help them, amen." After that, I went to say Mass at St. Thomas More Church. I went to the foyer to greet the people when it was over. I saw a couple drive into the parking lot. They approached me and handed me an envelope saying, "Father, we were praying this morning, and the Lord asked us to go and give you some money, that you needed it." When I opened the envelope, I saw that $2,500 was in it! God knows all our needs, and that's why in Matthew's gospel, he said, "Do not worry about what you will eat or what you will wear for your heavenly Father knows that you need them. Seek you first the kingdom of God, and every other thing will be added unto to you" (Matthew 6:25-33).

Jesus: my friend and everything

In John's gospel, Jesus said to his apostles, "I no longer call you servants because a servant does not know what his master is doing. I call you friends because I have made known to you everything I have learned from my father" (John 15:15). We can have two types of relationships with Jesus and God – a servant or slave relationship and a friend or son relationship. A servant doesn't have rights and privileges, but a son or friend has. Jesus wants us to have a friend-friend relationship. That's the image of Jesus that I have when I come to him in prayer. I know he loves and cares for me, so I trust him completely. I share everything going on in my life with him and, just like my friends will do anything they can to help me when in need, I know Jesus will do everything I ask him if he knows it's for my good. He is my best friend, my dad, and my confidant. He knows everything about me even before I think about it. Because of that, I don't need to panic or worry. I know he is in control. He has never failed me before, and I know he never will. He brings people into my life when I need them in such a mysterious way that confirms that he had a plan for me even before I came into being. My life is not an accident. There is no coincidence in God's plan. A Spanish adage says, "Ninguna hoja se mueve sin que Dios lo permita," which means, "No leaf can move if God doesn't allow it." I believe that my life is in God's hands, and whatever he does not allow will never happen, and whatever he does allow will be for my good in the long run.

I have witnessed God's hand in everything in my life, including in the writing of this book. When I first thought of publishing it, I decided to give it to someone to read and give me feedback. I didn't know any editors, but I learned, in a conversation with a parishioner, that her brother had written two books, and perhaps he could be of help. I called her brother and arranged for a meeting. He told me that, by profession, he is an engineer, not an editor, but he could put me in touch with the woman who helped him when he published one of his books. It turned out that I had once met her and her husband. We have several things in common, including that they speak Spanish and have lived and worked in Latin America. She kindly agreed to edit the book for me and made valuable suggestions that resulted in the making of two books rather than just one. I am very grateful. As I said to her and all those who support our work, "If you ever wonder what your mission in life is, please know that coming into my life is one of them and, because of you, my life and ministry are blessed, happier and richer."

As I wondered whether to go ahead with the publication or not, she said something that not only gave me courage but also confirmed what I prayed for. Before I started writing, I prayed to God in these words, "Lord Jesus, I am not writing this book for fame or money but to acknowledge and testify to your goodness and mercy in my life as I celebrate twenty-five years of priesthood. Thank you and be praised for all you have done in me and through me. Holy Spirit, touch my heart and the hearts of anyone who reads this book so that they may be inspired to look back and see your hand at work in the different circumstances and experiences of their life. May the readers be encouraged in their journey of faith, appreciate God's goodness, be open to the promptings of the Holy Spirit and become instruments of God's love and mercy." And she told me it helped do exactly that for her.

I often don't know how to tell people how awesome God is and how to trust him completely. It is a blessing to have a close relationship with him. If you've never experienced his merciful love, I encourage you never to give up. Speak to him from your heart and listen to him respond to you. He may speak to you in his Word, through another person or an event in your life. At all times, I go to him through prayer and his Word. In this way, I stay connected with him, and he gives me inner peace and joy.

Even if the whole world seems to be falling apart, I am not worried because “Greater is he who is in me than he who is in the world” (1 John 4:4-5).

Suggested action: Pray with Psalm 23 and the Gospel of Matthew 6:25-34.

Prayer: Lord Jesus, please take care of me and all my needs – both seen and unseen. I trust completely in you as my Good Shepherd and Divine provider, and there’s nothing I shall want. Amen!

13

Remaining connected

It is often said that life is a journey filled with ups and downs. I certainly have experienced those ups and downs as I journey along the way. Living in Canada is a great blessing, though not without its challenges. One of the struggles here in Canada and our contemporary society is staying connected with God without being carried away by social trends and the constant activity in a changing world. One needs to be very careful, intentional and focused on avoiding being engulfed by the waves of secularism and materialism. Among the things that have helped me maintain a connection with God is prayer. Growing up, I learned that prayer is a conversation with God. I didn't quite understand it then, but as I advance in this journey with the Lord I am trying to learn and grow in the art of having a quality conversation and communion with him. I have discovered that, when I maintain a regular prayer life, I am more at peace; I am happier and more focused. When I neglect my prayer life, I tend to be weak and distracted.

Among the prayers that have helped me maintain my faith and connection with God, with Jesus and the Holy Spirit are the Holy Mass, the Holy Rosary and the Divine Mercy Chaplet. Adoration of the Most Blessed Sacrament is a comfort to me. Sometimes, I do Lectio Divina and I practice the prayer of presence and silence, which is simply staying silent or quiet in adoration before

Jesus in the Blessed Sacrament. I gaze at him, and he gazes at me. His gaze is always soothing. Sometimes I listen to praise and worship songs or play some songs with my guitar. Songs like:

Goodness of God by Jenn Johnson

Promises by Joel Barnes and Naomi Raine

Reckless Love by Cory

Goodness, Love and Mercy by Chris Tomlin

The Blessing by Kari Jobe and Cody Carnes

No Longer Slaves by Bethel Music

Our God Saves by Paul Baloche

Excess Love by Mercy Chinwo

What a Beautiful Name by Hillsong

When It's All Been Said and Done by Robin Mark

Chineke m idi mma and *A Heart Full of Gratitude* by Fr. Toochukwu Okafor from his music CD titled *Love, The Universal Language.*

Being in such union of mind and heart with the Divine can inspire a lot of positive experiences. I must say that the production of my music CD was born out of a series of these experiences, which I consider providential. When I was a postulant in my first year in the seminary, I could not sing very well, and our Postulant Master used to call me "Volume 10" – meaning that my voice was very deep and loud – so he always asked me to sing bass. Since we took turns singing the

Liturgy of the Hours (Psalms) every day, I practiced continuously to ensure I didn't make mistakes. "Practice makes perfect" and, gradually, I began to improve. When I went to Bigard Memorial Seminary in Enugu, one of my classmates was an excellent guitarist. I loved to hear him play, and I desired to play like him. During recreation, I would go to him to learn. He taught me a few chords and, with those, I started playing some simple songs. Each time, before I started practicing, I would pray to the Holy Spirit and ask for help, promising to use whatever little music I learned to praise God, and that was precisely what I did. I always played the little I knew in thanksgiving and joyful praise to God. After all, my name, Toochukwu, means "Praise God."

One thing I learned from that experience is the power of desire. Whenever you have a desire or a dream to do something good, no matter how difficult or impossible it seems, don't give up. Start from somewhere, no matter how little. Even when you make mistakes or people laugh at you as they did at me, if you persistently keep practicing without giving up and continue to pray for God's help, you will surely make a breakthrough and achieve your goal. It is said that a journey of a thousand miles starts with a single step. The worst thing that can happen to you is to die without living out your dreams or at least attempting to live them out. So, never give up because of fear or because you are feeling inadequate and weak. My desire to learn the guitar and use it to praise God and remain connected to him finally bore fruit when I least expected it, all to the glory and praise of God.

Earlier in this book, I spoke about the power of encouragement. It is a virtue I encourage you to develop. Always try to encourage others to bring out the best in them; you never know the positive impact that will make in their lives.

In 2013 when I was at St. Genevieve parish, East Chezzetcook, the secretary, Mary Colford, heard me playing my guitar and joyfully singing praises to the Lord. She invited me to sing a song at the annual parish fall fair and music concert. At first, I didn't want to accept the invitation because I didn't feel competent to perform before the public. She insisted and continuously encouraged me to do it. Eventually, I accepted the invitation because I felt it was one way of identifying with the community and supporting the fundraising events for the good of the parish. Then thinking of what to sing, I was inspired to write a song to express how I feel about the love, kindness, hospitality, and support I have received from so many people since I came to this great country, Canada, particularly in Nova Scotia. Hence, I wrote the song, *I Love You Nova Scotia,* which I dedicated to all the beautiful Nova Scotians. After performing the song, I received great feedback and was encouraged to record it. That motivated me to write a few more songs, including *God Bless All Mothers of the World*" (dedicated to all mothers and women), *It Is My Birthday* to mark my fiftieth birthday, *I Will Praise Him Forevermore* and *The Knights of Columbus Honour You* dedicated to Blessed Michael J. McGivney the Founder of the Knights of Columbus. One of our parishioners, John Anderson, a musician, helped me arrange the songs.

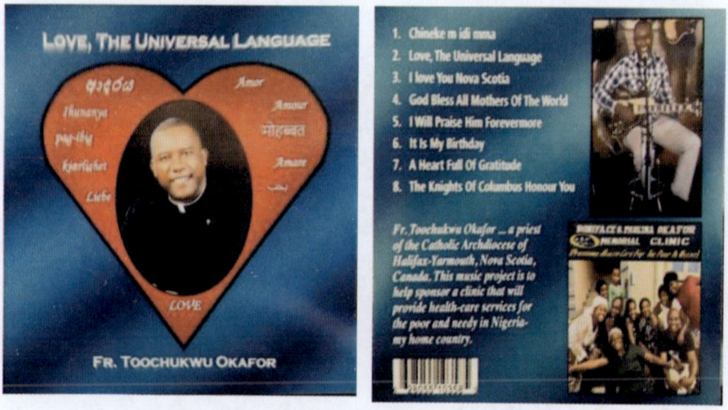

The CD with music and performance by Father Toochukwu Okafor

When I came to St. Thomas More Church, I sang *I Love You Nova Scotia* at one of the community gatherings – a multicultural fiesta – and everyone seemed to love it. After that, the BAPOM hospital and Family Care Program coordinators encouraged me to record it so that the proceeds could go to support our medical clinic project and the low-income families in Nigeria. I am grateful to God and those who encouraged me and helped in the production. Whenever I sing any of my songs, it connects me with God and the beautiful people I have met in the different parishes and communities I have served.

In the spiritual journey, every day is not Christmas. I am not always concentrated, nor do I always find it easy to pray. I do have my time of spiritual dryness and distractions, so I constantly look for ways to stay focused and connected to the source of my life and joy. Another thing that helps me when I get distracted is spiritual reading. I find Sarah Young's book – *Jesus*

Calling: Enjoying Peace in His Presence and *The Imitation of Christ* by Thomas A. Kempis very helpful, soothing, inspiring, and uplifting. Reading spiritual books helps elevate the mind and soul and inspires us to draw closer to God, to Jesus and the Holy Spirit. It is left for the individual to find a book that appeals to you depending on the circumstances you are going through at the time. It would be great for everyone to try reading at least one spiritual book a year; you never know how that will impact your life and make you a better person. Some of our parishioners who are experiencing book study testify to how enlightening and enriching it is to their minds, souls and bodies. They always look forward to it.

In terms of pastoral ministry, reading the books *Divine Renovation: Bringing Your Parish from Maintenance to Mission* by Father James Mallon and *Rebuilt*: *Awakening the Faithful, Reaching the Lost, and Making Church Matter* by Michael White and Tom Corcoran reawakened my missionary zeal and desire to work for the renewal of the Church. The promotion of new evangelization and reaching the lost and those on the periphery is at the heart of the Gospel and the mission of the Church. Learning the principles of leading as a Team and sharing experiences with other clergies, which is one of the critical components of Divine Renovation Network, has helped me remain connected with God, the priesthood, and Christ's faithful. It has been a saving grace for me in my ministry. The same leadership structure was introduced in the Archdiocese of Halifax-Yarmouth by Archbishop Emeritus Anthony Mancini and supported by Archbishop Brian Dunn when we started restructuring the diocese with the amalgamation of our parishes. These are aimed at parish and Diocesan renewal, which Pope Francis encouraged in his book *The Joy of the Gospel.*

Reading Pope Francis' writings has helped me to remain focused on seeking to do the will of God and promoting Christ's mission and not focusing only on my preferences. Having the opportunity to celebrate and pray with the faithful of our community and the various religious groups or ministries in the parish gives me life spiritually, emotionally and mentally. I meet Christ in our parishioners who encourage me in my faith journey.

The Word of God as our guide

As we journey along the road of life, we don't always know what we will encounter. Sometimes, the road is foggy and convoluted and we need a guide. When I go through different emotions and challenges, I intentionally seek comfort in the Word of God because I believe it has the power to heal and give hope. In his prologue, John said, "In the beginning was the Word, and the Word was God, and the Word was with God, and the Word took flesh and dwelt among us" (John 1:1-5.) It is through that Word that all things were made. Through the Word of God, he comes to be with us and dwell in us as he dwelt in the womb of our Blessed Mother Mary. In the Word of God, there are many blessings and promises. It is left to us to take advantage of his words in whatever situation we may find ourselves.

I had an experience in 2004, when I was in Colombia, that made me truly appreciate the importance of claiming the promises of God in his Word. A friend of mine, Jenny, was sick with cancer and needed some money to go for chemotherapy. She asked me if I would help. I called one of our benefactors who agreed to help. She deposited one million Colombian pesos into Jenny's bank account – a substantial amount. When, after a month, I saw Jenny and asked her how the treatment went, she replied, "I have not received it; I was unable to raise the money." I called the benefactor and inquired if she had fulfilled her promise. She said that she had deposited the money into Jenny's account the same day we first spoke. Unfortunately, due to a miscommunication, Jenny didn't know it, so she suffered all that time even though she had money in the bank. If she had known and gone to the bank, she could have withdrawn the money and gone for her treatment earlier. What connection does this story have with the Word of God? In the Bible, God has deposited many blessings and promises for us. Sometimes, because we don't know about these promises, we don't claim them, so we continue to suffer and wander around in the dark. That's why St. Jerome said that "Ignorance of scripture is ignorance of God." If we only knew all the blessings and promises God has in store for us in his Word, we would make the Bible our constant companion and go to it to draw strength and guidance in whatever situation we might find ourselves. We would not suffer so many attacks by our adversary. Here are some scriptural passages that have helped me; perhaps you might find them helpful when you are feeling:

Anguished

To be anguished is to experience severe indescribable mental or physical pain, agony, or suffering. Jesus had such an experience in his agony in the garden. At such moments, the only one who perfectly understands you is God. Hence turning to his word can bring comfort and peace. The Psalmist says, "In my distress, I called to the Lord; he answered me and set me free. The Lord is with me; I will not be afraid; what can anyone do to me? The Lord helps me, and I will see my enemies defeated. It is better to trust in the Lord than to depend on human beings. It is better to trust in the Lord than to depend on human leaders" (Psalm 118: 5-9).

The Lord never fails those who put their trust in him. Thus, you can confidently pray with Psalm 102:1-2, "Listen to my prayer, O Lord, and hear my cry for help! When I am in trouble, don't turn away from me! Listen to me and answer me quickly when I call!"

"I love the Lord because he hears me; he listens to my prayers. He listens to me every time I call him. The danger of death was all around me; the horrors of the grave closed in on me; I was filled with fear and anxiety. Then I called to the Lord, "I beg you, Lord, save me!" The Lord is merciful and good; our God is compassionate. The Lord protects the helpless; when I was in danger, he saved me. Be confident, my heart, because the Lord has been good to me. The Lord saved me from death; he stopped my tears and kept me from defeat. And so, I walk in the presence of the Lord in the land of the living. I kept on believing, even when I said, "I am completely crushed," even when I was afraid and said, "No one can be trusted" (Psalm 116: 1-11).

"To you, O Lord, I offer my prayer; in you, my God, I trust. Save me from the shame of defeat; don't let my enemies gloat over me! Turn to me, Lord, and be merciful to me because I am lonely and weak. Relieve me of my worries and save me from all my troubles. Consider my distress and suffering and forgive all my sins" (Psalm 25: 1-3, 16- 18).

"Listen to me, Lord, and answer me, for I am helpless and weak. Save me from death, because I am loyal to you; save me, for I am your servant and I trust in you. You are my God, so be merciful to me; I pray to you all day long. Make your servant glad, O Lord, because my prayers go up to you. You are good to us and forgiving, full of constant love for all who pray to you. Listen, Lord, to my prayer; hear my cries for help. I call to you in times of trouble because you answer my prayers. There is no god like you, O Lord, not one has done what you have done" (Psalm 86:1-8).

"The Lord is a refuge for the oppressed, a place of safety in times of trouble. Those who know you, Lord, will trust you; you do not abandon anyone who comes to you" (Psalm 9:9-10).

"The Lord is my protector; he is my strong fortress. My God is my protection, and with him I am safe. He protects me like a shield; he defends me and keeps me safe. He is my saviour; he protects me and saves me from violence. I call to the Lord, and he saves me from my enemies. Praise the Lord. The waves of death were all around me; the waves of destruction rolled over me. The danger of death was around me, and the grave set its trap for me. In my trouble I called to the Lord; I called to my God for help. In his temple he heard my voice; he listened to my cry for help" (2 Samuel 22:2-7).

"Do not be afraid, I am with you! I am your God let nothing terrify you! I will make you strong and help you; I will protect you and save you" (Isaiah 41:10).

"Don't you know? Haven't you heard? The Lord is the everlasting God; he created all the world. He never grows tired or weary. No one understands his thoughts. He strengthens those who are weak and tired. Even those who are young grow weak; young people can fall exhausted. But those who trust in the Lord for help will find their strength renewed. They will rise on wings like eagles; they will run and not get weary; they will walk and not grow weak" (Isaiah 40:28-31).

What wonderful promises given by the Lord! He is faithful to his promises. All we need is to take his Word seriously and call upon Him with faith and trust.

Depressed

One of the most common mental health illnesses that people experience today is depression, a mood disorder that causes a constant and prolonged feeling of sadness and loss of interest. If you are experiencing either a mild or major depression, it may affect how you feel, think and behave, leading to various emotional and physical problems. You may have trouble doing normal daily activities and, sometimes, you may feel as if your life is not worth living. Sometimes you may require medication or psychotherapy to get things under control. However, turning to the Word of God and applying it to your life can help lift the spirit, mind, and body. At such moments you can pray with the Palmist:

"Hear my cry, O God; listen to my prayer! In despair and far from home, I call to you! Take me to a safe refuge, for you are my protector, my strong defense against my enemies. Let me live in your sanctuary all my life; let me find safety under your wings" (Psalm 61:1-4). Take a moment to meditate on these words and imagine God covering you with his protective arms, enveloping you with his love and peace.

"I look to the mountains; where will my help come from? My help will come from the Lord, who made heaven and earth. He will not let you fall; your protector is always awake. The protector of Israel never dozes or sleeps. The Lord will guard you; he is by your side to protect you. The sun will not hurt you during the day, nor the moon during the night. The Lord will protect you from all danger; he will keep you safe. He will protect you as you come and go now and forever" (Psalm 121:1-8).

"The righteous call to the Lord, and he listens; he rescues them from all their troubles. The Lord is near to those who are discouraged; he saves those who have lost all hope. Good people suffer many troubles, but the Lord saves them from them all; the Lord preserves them completely; not one of their bones is broken. Evil will kill the wicked; those who hate the righteous will be punished. The Lord will save his people; those who go to him for protection will be spared" (Psalm 34: 17-22).

"Praise the Lord, my soul! All my being, praise his holy name! Praise the Lord, my soul, and do not forget how kind he is. He forgives all my sins and heals all my diseases. He keeps me from the grave and blesses me with love and mercy. He fills my life with good things to stay young and strong like an eagle. The Lord judges in favour of the oppressed and gives them their rights. He revealed his plans to Moses and let the people of Israel see his mighty deeds. The Lord is merciful and loving, slow to become angry and full of constant love" (Psalm 103: 1-8).

"O God, you are my God, and I long for you. My whole being desires you; like a dry, worn-out, and waterless land, my soul is thirsty for you. Let me see you in the sanctuary; let me see how mighty and glorious you are. Your constant love is better than life itself, and so I will praise you. I will give you thanks as long as I live; I will raise my hands to you in prayer. My soul will feast and be satisfied, and I will sing glad songs of praise to you. As I lie in bed, I remember you; I think of you all night long because you have always been my help. In the shadow of your wings, I sing for joy. I cling to you, and your hand keeps me safe" (Psalm 63:1-8).

"I waited patiently for the Lord's help; then, he listened to me and heard my cry. He pulled me out of a dangerous pit, out of the deadly quicksand. He set me safely on a rock and made me secure. He taught me to sing a new song, praise to our God. Many who see this will take warning and will put their trust in the Lord. Happy are those who trust the Lord, who do not turn to idols or join those who worship false gods. You have done many things for us, O Lord our God; there is no one like you! You have made many wonderful plans for us. I could never speak of them all; their number is so great" (Psalm 40:1-5)!

Experience shows that whenever we are going through rough times, we tend to be impatient; we want the problem to be resolved instantly. This is because no one likes to suffer. However, after you have prayed and put everything into God's hands, you must learn to wait on the Lord patiently. He listens to all our prayers and grants all our petitions, but his time frame and how he answers may be different from our expectations. So, we pray and trust that he will give us what is best for he is our loving Father.

"Israel, (or replace Israel with your name) the Lord who created you says, "Do not be afraid. I will save you. I have called you by name; you are mine. When you pass through deep waters, I will be with you; your troubles will not overwhelm you. When you pass through the fire, you will not be burnt; the hard trials that come will not hurt you, for I am the Lord your God, the holy God of Israel, who saves you. I will give up Egypt to set you free; I will give up Ethiopia and Sheba. I will give up whole nations to save your life, because you are precious to me and because I love you and give you honour. Do not be afraid. I am with you" (Isaiah 43:1-5)!

"The Lord has filled me with his Spirit. He has chosen me and sent me to bring good news to the poor, to heal the broken-hearted, to announce release to captives and freedom to those in prison. He has sent me to proclaim that the time has come when the Lord will save his people and defeat their enemies. He has sent me to comfort all who mourn, to give to those who mourn in Zion, joy and gladness instead of grief, a song of praise instead of sorrow" (Isaiah 61:1-3).

"For I am convinced that neither death nor life, neither angels nor demons, neither the present nor the future, nor any powers, neither height nor depth, nor anything else in all creation, will be able to separate us from the love of God that is in Christ Jesus our Lord" (Romans 8:38-3).

"We are often troubled, but not crushed; sometimes in doubt, but never in despair; there are many enemies, but we are never without a friend; and though badly hurt at times, we are not destroyed. At all times we carry in our mortal bodies the death of Jesus, so that his life also may be seen in our bodies" (2 Corinthians 4:8-10).

"My dear friends, do not be surprised at the painful test you are suffering, as though something unusual was happening to you. Rather be glad that you are sharing Christ's sufferings, so that you may be full of joy when his glory is revealed" (1 Peter 4:12-13).

"Humble yourselves, then, under God's mighty hand, so that he will lift you in his own good time. Leave all your worries with him because he cares for you. Be alert, be on the watch! Your enemy, the Devil, roams around like a roaring lion, looking for someone to devour. Be firm in your faith and resist him because you know that your fellow believers in all the world are going through the same kind of suffering. But after you have suffered for a little while, the God of all grace, who calls you to share his eternal glory in union with Christ, will himself perfect you and give you firmness, strength, and a sure foundation. To him be the power forever! Amen" (1 Peter 5:6-11).

"From Paul, an apostle of Christ Jesus by God's will, and from our brother Timothy to the church of God in Corinth, and to all God's people throughout Achaia: May God our Father and the Lord Jesus Christ give you grace and peace. Let us give thanks to the God and Father of our Lord Jesus Christ, the merciful Father, the God from whom all help comes! He helps us in all our troubles so that we can help others who have all kinds of troubles, using the same help that we have received from God. Just as we have a share in Christ's many sufferings, so also through Christ we share in God's great help" (2 Corinthians 1:1-5).

"Given all this, what can we say? If God is for us, who can be against us? Certainly not God, who did not even keep back his own Son, but offered him for us all! He gave us his Son; will he not also freely give us all things? Who will accuse God's chosen people? God himself declares them not guilty! Who, then, will condemn them?

Not Christ Jesus, who died, or rather, who was raised to life and is at the right-hand side of God, pleading with him for us! Who, then, can separate us from the love of Christ? Can trouble do it, or hardship or persecution or hunger or poverty or danger or death" (Romans 8:31)?

"Let your hope keep you joyful, be patient in your troubles, and pray at all times" (Romans 12:12).

Discouraged

There are so many things that can bring discouragement. No matter what it is, bring it to the Lord in prayer and listen attentively to his Words so that you may find peace and encouragement to move ahead in the journey of life. Hear the Lord say to you,

"Be glad about this, even though it may now be necessary for you to be sad for a while because of the many kinds of trials you suffer. Their purpose is to prove that your faith is genuine. Even gold, which can be destroyed, is tested by fire; and so, your faith, which is much more precious than gold, must also be tested so that it may endure. Then you will receive praise and glory and honour on the Day when Jesus Christ is revealed. Although you have not seen him, you love him and believe in him. So, you rejoice with a great and glorious joy which words cannot express because you are receiving the salvation of your souls, which is the purpose of your faith in him" (1 Peter 1:6-9).

"Don't worry about anything, but in all your prayers, ask God for what you need, always asking him with a thankful heart. And God's peace, which is far beyond human understanding, will keep your hearts and minds safe in union with Christ Jesus. In conclusion, my brothers and sisters, fill your minds with those things that are good and that deserve praise: things that are true, noble, right, pure, lovely, and honourable" (Philippians 4: 6-8).

"I have the strength to face all conditions by the power that Christ gives me" (Philippians 4: 13).

"When you pass through deep waters, I will be with you; your troubles will not overwhelm you. When you pass through the fire, you will not be burnt; the hard trials that come will not hurt you" (Isaiah 43: 2).

"So, let us not become tired of doing good; for if we do not give up, the time will come when we will reap the harvest" (Galatians 6: 9).

"My dear friends, do not be surprised at the painful test you are suffering, as though something unusual was happening to you. Rather be glad that you are sharing Christ's sufferings, so that you may be full of joy when his glory is revealed" (1 Peter 4: 12-13).

"Three times, I prayed to the Lord about this and asked him to take it away. But his answer was: My grace is all you need, for my power is greatest when you are weak. I am most happy, then, to be proud of my weaknesses, to feel the protection of Christ's power over me. I am content with weaknesses, insults, hardships, persecutions, and difficulties, for Christ's sake. When I am weak, I am strong" (2 Corinthians 12:8-10).

Angry

Anger is one of the basic human emotions. It is good to express your anger and not repress it. However, the way you handle your anger matters a lot. In Ephesians 4:26, St. Paul says, "Be angry but do not sin; do not let the sun go down on your anger, and do not make room for the devil." In other words, moderate expression of anger can help let the other person know their limit and can help to create a boundary. But if your anger leads to prolonged aggression verbally or physically or resentment, it becomes sinful. The following passages of scripture may help you control yourself when you feel angry.

"Be patient and wait for the LORD to act; don't be worried about those who prosper or those who succeed in their evil plans. Don't give in to worry or anger; it only leads to trouble. Those who trust in the LORD will possess the land, but the wicked will be driven out" (Psalm 37:7-9).

"Keep your temper under control; it is foolish to harbour a grudge" (Ecclesiastes 7:9).

"Get rid of all bitterness, passion, and anger. No more shouting or insults, no more hateful feelings of any sort. Instead, be kind and tender-hearted to one another, and forgive one another, as God has forgiven you through Christ" (Ephesians 4:31-32).

"Remember this, my dear brothers and sisters! Everyone must be quick to listen, but slow to speak and slow to become angry. Human anger does not achieve God's righteous purpose" (James 1: 19-20).

"If you become angry, do not let your anger lead you into sin, and do not stay angry all day" (Ephesians 4:26).

"A gentle answer quiets anger, but a harsh one stirs it up" (Proverbs 15: 1).

"If you forgive others the wrongs they have done to you, your Father in heaven will also forgive you" (Matthew 6: 14).

"Never take revenge, my friends, but instead let God's anger do it. For the scripture says, "I will take revenge, I will pay back, says the Lord" (Romans 12:19).

"It is better to be patient than powerful. It is better to win control over yourself than over whole cities" (Proverbs 16:32).

"If your enemies are hungry, feed them; if they are thirsty, give them a drink. You will make them burn with shame, and the LORD will reward you" (Proverbs 25:21-22).

"But now you must get rid of all these things: anger, passion, and hateful feelings. No insults or obscene talk must ever come from your lips. Do not lie to one another, for you have taken off the old self with its habits and have put on the new self… You are the people of God; he loved you and chose you for his own. So then, you must clothe yourselves with compassion, kindness, humility, gentleness, and patience. Be tolerant with one another and forgive one another whenever any of you has a complaint against someone else. You must forgive one another just as the Lord has forgiven you. And to all these qualities add love, which binds all things together in perfect unity. The peace that Christ gives is to guide you in your decisions; for it is to this peace that God has called you together in the one body. And be thankful" (Colossians 12:8-15).

"But I say to you that whoever is angry with his brother without a cause shall be in danger of the judgment. And whoever says to his brother, 'you are good for nothing' shall be in danger of the council. But whoever says 'you fool' shall be in danger of hellfire. Therefore, if you bring your gift to the altar, remember that, if your brother has something against you, leave your gift there before the altar and go your way. First, be reconciled to your brother, and then come and offer your gift" (Matthew 5: 22-24).

Impatient

Impatience refers to restlessness or shortness of temper especially anxiety when there is a delay. How do you feel when you have to wait for something for a long time? Do you feel anxious, frustrated, crazy, or impatient? Being impatient can have so many negative consequences on your life and relationships. Therefore, it is of great benefit to your spiritual and emotional well-being if you can cultivate the virtue of patience. This requires self-control which is one of the greatest gifts of the Holy Spirit. Because it is a gift, you need to pray for it and wait to receive it. Sometimes, when you pray for the gift of patience, God will allow you to face some challenging situations or deal with difficult people, which is how you acquire the gift of patience. You can only know you have the gift of patience when exposed to those challenging situations and handle them calmly. So, if you're impatient and want to grow in patience, it might be helpful to reflect and pray with the following Bible passages.

"May you be made strong with all the strength which comes from his glorious power, so that you may be able to endure everything with patience. And with joy give thanks to the Father, who has made you fit to have your share of what God has reserved for his people in the kingdom of light" (Colossians 1:11-12).

"Be patient and wait for the Lord to act; don't be worried about those who prosper or those who succeed in their evil plans. Don't give in to worry or anger; it only leads to trouble. Those who trust in the Lord will possess the land, but the wicked will be driven out" (Psalm 37: 7-9).

"What I say is this: let the Spirit direct your lives, and you will not satisfy the desires of the human nature. What our human nature wants is opposed to what the Spirit wants, and what the Spirit wants is opposed to what our human nature wants. These two are enemies, which means that you cannot do what you want. If the Spirit leads you, you are not subject to the Law. What human nature does is quite plain! It shows itself in immoral, filthy, indecent actions, idols' worship, and witchcraft. People become enemies and fight; they become jealous, angry, and ambitious. They separate into parties and groups; they are envious, get drunk, have orgies, and do things like these. I warn you now as I have before: those who do these things will not possess the Kingdom of God. But the Spirit produces love, joy, peace, patience, kindness, goodness, faithfulness, humility, and self-control. There is no law against such things as these" (Galatians 5:16-23).

"For you know that when your faith succeeds in facing such trials, the result is the ability to endure. Make sure that your endurance carries you without failing, so that you may be perfect and complete, lacking nothing" (James 1: 3-4).

"The end of anything is better than its beginning. Patience is better than pride. Keep your temper under control; it is foolish to harbour a grudge" (Ecclesiastes 7: 8-9).

"Be patient, then, my friends, until the Lord comes. See how patient farmers are as they wait for their land to produce precious crops. They wait patiently for the autumn and spring rains. You also must be patient. Keep your hopes high, for the day of the Lord's coming is nearby. Do not complain against one another, my friends, so that God will not judge you. The Judge is near, ready to appear. My friends, remember the prophets who spoke in the name of the Lord. Take them as examples of patient endurance under suffering. We call them happy because they endured. You have heard of Job's patience, and you know how the Lord provided for him in the end. For the Lord is full of mercy and compassion" (James 5:7-11).

"We also boast of our troubles because we know that trouble produces endurance, endurance brings God's approval, and his approval creates hope. This hope does not disappoint us, for God has poured out his love into our hearts using the Holy Spirit, who is God's gift to us" (Romans 5:3-5).

Dissatisfied

Are you satisfied with the life you're living? Are you satisfied with how things are going in your family, marriage or relationships? It is possible that you may not be pleased or satisfied with everything right now. And that is okay. You are allowed to feel discontent or dissatisfied and to express it. However, it is good to know that you can share those feelings with God, your loving Father. He can help you change your perception about whatever experience makes you feel dissatisfied and give you contentment and peace. And you will be able to say with the Psalmist, "Praise the Lord, my soul! All my being, praise his holy name! He forgives all my sins and heals all my diseases. He keeps me from the grave and blesses me with love and mercy. He fills my life with good things to stay young and strong like an eagle" (Psalm 103: 1-5).

"They must thank the Lord for his constant love, for the wonderful things he did for them. He satisfies those who are thirsty and fills the hungry with good things" (Psalm 107:8-9).

"And I will always guide you and satisfy you with good things. I will keep you strong and well. You will be like a garden that has plenty of water, like a spring of water that never runs dry. Your people will rebuild what has long been in ruins, building again on the old foundations. You will be known as the people who rebuilt the walls, who restored the ruined houses" (Isaiah 58:11-12).

"And God can give you more than you need so that you will always have all you need for yourselves and more than enough for every good cause. As the scripture says: "He gives generously to the needy; his kindness lasts forever" (2 Corinthians 9:8-9).

"Trust in the LORD and do good; live in the land and be safe. Seek your happiness in the Lord and he will give you your heart's desire. Give yourself to the Lord; trust in him, and he will help you" (Psalm 37:3-5).

"I know what it is to be in need and what it is to have more than enough. I have learned this secret, so that anywhere, at any time, I am content, whether I am full or hungry, whether I have too much or too little. I have the strength to face all conditions by the power that Christ gives me" (Philippians 4:12-13).

Insecure

One of the things we desire most is security at different levels of our lives. When we feel any aspect of our life is in jeopardy, we lose our peace of mind. At such moments, scripture reminds us that we have a Father who is a Good Shepherd who cares for us and can protect us from anything, seen and unseen, that can threaten our life. We need to run to him and trust that he will protect us from all harm and provide for all we need. Praying with the following Bible passages could be helpful.

"The Lord is my Shepherd; there is nothing I shall want. He makes me lie down in green pastures. He leads me beside still waters. He restores my soul. He leads me on the right paths for his name's sake. Even though I walk through the darkest valley, I fear no evil; For you are with me; your rod and your staff – they comfort me. You prepare a table before me in the presence of my enemies; you anoint my head with oil, my cup overflows. Surely goodness and mercy shall follow me all the days of my life and I shall dwell in the house of the Lord my whole life long" (Psalm 23).

"When you pass through deep waters, I will be with you; your troubles will not overwhelm you. When you pass through the fire, you will not be burnt; the hard trials that come will not hurt you, for I am the Lord your God, the holy God of Israel, who saves you. I will give up Egypt to set you free; I will give up Ethiopia and Sheba" (Isaiah 43:2-3).

"I am the Lord your God; I strengthen you and say, 'Do not be afraid; I will help you" (Isaiah 41:13).

"Let us be bold, then, and say: "The Lord is my helper, I will not be afraid. What can anyone do to me" (Hebrews 13:6)?

"For I am certain that nothing can separate us from his love: neither death nor life, neither angels nor other heavenly rulers or powers, neither the present nor the future, neither the world above nor the world below, nor anything else in all creation will ever be able to separate us from the love of God which is ours through Christ Jesus our Lord" (Romans 8:38-39).

"But the Lord is faithful, and he will strengthen you and keep you safe from the evil one" (Thessalonians 3:3).

Worried/Anxious

Often, things don't go the way we want them to. If you are the type who worries about everything, don't feel bad about it. It shows that you care. However, it is important to remember that no matter how much we worry and get anxious, it may not resolve our problem; it may even worsen it. This confirms an adage that says, "Preoccupation only brings tiredness. It doesn't resolve your problem." The good news is that you and I have someone who can resolve all our problems. Therefore, scripture encourages us to bring all our worries and anxiety to him, and he will take care of them.

"Humble yourselves, then, under God's mighty hand, so that he will lift you in his own good time. Leave all your worries with him because he cares for you" (1 Peter 5:6-7).

"Give yourself to the LORD; trust in him, and he will help you; he will make your righteousness shine like the noonday sun" (Psalm 37:5-6).

"So, do not worry and say: 'What are we going to eat? What are we going to drink? Or what shall we wear? The Gentiles busy themselves with such things; but your heavenly Father knows that you need them all. Set your hearts first on the Kingdom of God and his justice and all these things will also be given to you. Do not worry about tomorrow for tomorrow will worry about itself. Each day has enough trouble of its own" (Matthew 6: 31-34 - NCB).

"Show a gentle attitude towards everyone. The Lord is coming soon. Don't worry about anything, but in all your prayers ask God for what you need, always asking him with a thankful heart. And God's peace, which is far beyond human understanding, will keep your hearts and minds safe in union with Christ Jesus" (Philippians 4:5-7).

And with all his abundant wealth through Christ Jesus, my God will supply all your needs" (Philippians 4:19).

"The peace that Christ gives is to guide you in the decisions you make; for it is to this peace that God has called you together in the one body. And be thankful. Christ's message in all its richness must live in your hearts. Teach and instruct each other with all wisdom. Sing psalms, hymns, and sacred songs; sing to God with thanksgiving in your hearts. Everything you do or say, then, should be done in the name of the Lord Jesus, as you give thanks through him to God the Father" (Colossians 3:15-17).

Lonely

One of the sicknesses many people suffer from in our society today is loneliness – the act of being without company. Even among married couples, some who, though they are living together in one house, still feel lonely. It is unfortunate to experience existential aloneness. Often it produces a feeling of bleakness or desolation. It is comforting to know that when everyone abandons you, there is someone who always walks with you along life's journey. He will always be with you, and he wants to accompany you at every moment. All you need is to be aware of his abiding presence and speak to him heart to heart. No matter what you do or where you go, he will not hide from you if only you let him accompany you. When you feel lonely or desolate, turn to him and pray with the Psalmist thus:

"Don't hide from me!" Don't be angry with me; don't turn your servant away. You have been my help; don't leave me, don't abandon me, O God, my Savior. My father and mother may abandon me, but the Lord will take care of me" (Psalms 27:9-10).

"I am always aware of the Lord's presence; he is near, and nothing can shake me" (Psalms 16:8).

"Do not be afraid – I am with you! I am your God – let nothing terrify you! I will make you strong and help you; I will protect you and save you" (Isaiah 41: 10).

"Remember, I will be with you and protect you wherever you go, and I will bring you back to this land. I will not leave you until I have done all that I have promised you." Jacob woke up and said, "The Lord is here! He is in this place, and I didn't know it" (Genesis 28:15-18).

"Jesus drew near and said to his disciples, "All authority in heaven and earth has been given to me by my Father. Go, therefore, to all peoples everywhere and make them my disciples: baptize them in the name of the Father, the Son, and the Holy Spirit, and teach them to obey everything I have commanded you. And I will be with you always, to the end of the age" (Matthew 38:18-20).

"Who, then, can separate us from the love of Christ? Can trouble do it, or hardship or persecution or hunger or poverty or danger or death? As the scripture says, "For your sake, we are in danger of death at all times; we are treated like sheep that are going to be slaughtered." No, in all these things we have complete victory through him who loved us! For I am certain that nothing can separate us from his love: neither death nor life, neither angels nor other heavenly rulers or powers, neither the present nor the future, neither the world above nor the world below; there is nothing in all creation that will ever be able to separate us from the love of God which is ours through Christ Jesus our Lord" (Romans 8:35-39).

"Be determined and confident. Do not be afraid of them. Your God, the Lord himself, will be with you. He will not fail you or abandon you" (Deuteronomy 31:6).

"God is our shelter and strength, always ready to help in times of trouble. So, we will not be afraid, even if the earth is shaken and mountains fall into the ocean depths" (Psalms 46:1-2).

"Keep your lives free from the love of money and be satisfied with what you have. For God has said, "I will never leave you; I will never abandon you" (Hebrews 13:5).

"So, the Lord answers, "Can a woman forget her baby and not love the child she bore? Even if a mother should forget her child, I will never forget you" (Isaiah 49:15).

"I alone know the plans I have for you, plans to bring you prosperity and not disaster, plans to bring about the future you hope for. Then you will call me. You will come and pray to me, and I will answer you. You will seek me, and you will find me because you will seek me with all your heart. Yes, I say, you will find me, and I will restore you to your land. I will gather you from every country and from every place to which I have scattered you, and I will bring you back to the land from which I had sent you away into exile. I, the Lord, have spoken" (Jeremiah 29:11-14).

Suggested action: Pray with some of the Bible quotations listed when experiencing these emotions. Take time to meditate on them and listen to God speak to you silently through them.

Prayer: Dear Jesus, when I go through the roller coaster of emotional turmoil, please help me to hear your gentle voice assuring me that you are with me and that with you I am more than a conqueror. Amen!

The freedom and joy of a good conscience

Would you like freedom, the joy of a good conscience, and peace of mind? The admonition of Thomas A. Kempis in chapter six of his book *The Imitation of Christ* is a secret that can help you achieve that. He said that the glory of a good person is the evidence of a good conscience. If you have a good conscience, you will always be happy. Having a good conscience enables you to bear all things and remain serene amid adversity.

On the contrary, a bad conscience makes you fearful and easily ruffled. You can only be glad when you have done well. Objectively speaking, evil persons are never really happy, nor do they feel peace within themselves, for "there is no peace for the wicked, says the Lord" (Isaiah 48:22). Although the wicked may project that peace is theirs and that no evil shall harm them, they know deep within their heart that peace has eluded them, so do not believe them. For God's wrath will suddenly overtake them. All they have done will be brought to nothing and their plans destroyed.

Those who love God will experience tribulation just like Jesus and the early Christians, but their sorrow will eventually lead to joy and glory on the cross of Jesus Christ, our Lord. The glory given and received by humans lasts a little while and is usually followed by sadness. The glory of good persons is in their conscience, not in the praise of others. The happiness of the good is in God, and their joy is in the truth. Those who long for true everlasting happiness do not care for that which is temporal. Those who seek temporal glory and do not treat it with contempt have little love for the joy of heaven. Those who are indifferent to praise or blame have great tranquility of heart.

People whose conscience is clear have peace and contentment. You are no better for being praised or worse for being blamed, for you are what you are, nor will you be more or less than God sees you. If you know what you are within yourself, the opinion of others will not interest you. "We see only the face, but God sees into the heart" (1 Sam 16:7). We look at the actions, but God considers the intentions. Always doing the best you can and making little of yourself is the mark of a humble soul. To refuse consolation from any creature shows cleanness of heart and confidence in God. Those who seek no outward testimony for themselves have committed themselves entirely to God. St. Paul says, “For it is not the one who commends himself who is approved, but the one whom the Lord commends” (2 Cor 10:18). Those who continually live intimately with God, not bound by any outward attachment, are in the state of an interior life.

14

We are of great value

One thing that is absolutely clear in my mind and heart is the conviction that we are chosen and loved by an infinite, all-powerful, loving, and merciful God. This is captured succinctly in St. Paul's letter to the Ephesians, which says,

> "Blessed be the God and Father of our Lord Jesus Christ, who has blessed us in Christ with every spiritual blessing in the heavenly places, just as he chose us in Christ before the foundation of the world to be holy and blameless before him in love. He destined us for adoption as his children through Jesus Christ, according to the good pleasure of his will, to the praise of his glorious grace that he freely bestowed on us in the Beloved. In him we have redemption through his blood, the forgiveness of our sins according to the riches of his grace that he lavished on us" (Ephesians 1:3-7 - NRSVB).

This passage reveals the fundamental truth that we didn't come into this life by accident. We are products of the infinite wisdom of God. He created us out of love and chose us to be his own. He made us weak so that, in our weakness, he might manifest his power, mercy, love, compassion, providence, and glory. Everything that has transpired in our lives from the moment of conception till death is known to him as expressed by the psalmist in Psalm 139, "Lord, you search me, and you know me.... For it was you who knit me together in my mother's womb." Also, Luke 12:7 says that you are so valuable that God has counted every hair on your head, and none will fall to the ground without his knowledge.

Awareness of this fundamental truth gives peace and comfort. Even when we are weak and fallen, we should remind ourselves of who we are, a child of God, adopted in Christ Jesus and washed in the precious blood of the Lamb. John's gospel, chapter 1:16, expressed it so well: "For God so loved the world that he gave his only Son that whoever believes in him shall not perish but will have eternal life."

If God can give his only son to die for us, it means we are of great value. Sometimes the world wants to belittle us or put us down; people may define us in numbers, functions, social class, race, colour, or gender. But it doesn't matter what others may think or say about us. What matters most is who and what God says about us. And he says that "You are chosen, adopted, and blessed with every spiritual blessing in the heavenly places." Do you believe this about yourself? If you do believe it, then you are a prince or princess. Therefore, do not let others define you because they do not know your value.

There is a story I read in the book *Orando y Viviendo* ("Praying and Living"), by Alberto Linero Gomez, about a young man who was sad and depressed because he felt no one loved him nor valued him. He went to a guru to seek counselling. The guru told him that he would like to help him but that, first, he had to attend to his wife, who was very sick. He would like to take her to the hospital but had no money. So, he asked the young man to help him by selling his gold ring. The young man agreed to sell it for him. When giving him the ring, the guru said, "Go to the marketplace and see if anyone is willing to buy it for $250 or more but don't sell it if they offer less than $250." The young man ran to the marketplace because he wanted to help the guru save his wife's life. He went everywhere in the market, but people were appraising the ring at only $50, $70, and up to $90. No one would pay $250. So, disappointed and exhausted from walking around the market seeking a prospective buyer, he sadly returned to the guru to report that he could not sell the ring. Then, the guru told him to go to the goldsmith who lived in the town and ask him how much he would be willing to pay for the ring. But he warned the young man not to sell the ring to the goldsmith. The young man was surprised because he knew that the guru needed money, so why would he tell him not to sell the ring? He ran to the goldsmith and said, "The master sent me to ask how much you are willing to pay for this ring." The goldsmith said, "I don't know what type of problem the master has to warrant him selling this precious treasure. Right now, I can offer $500, but if he gives me a few days to source for funds, I would be willing to pay $1000." The young man excitedly ran back to the guru with the good news. After telling the guru what the goldsmith had said, the guru said to the young man, "Did you notice that the ring was the same, but it received a different appraisal by different people. What happened to that ring is what is happening to you. When you took the ring to the marketplace, the people didn't know its true value; therefore, they underpriced it. But when you took it to the goldsmith who knew its value, he was willing to pay a higher price".

This can happen to us as well. We allow people who don't know our true value to put a low 'price tag' on us. How often have you let what people said about you demoralize you? Please do not give them that authority over you. God, who knows our true worth, was willing to pay the highest price to purchase our freedom and blessing through the death and resurrection of his only son, Jesus Christ. Can you begin today to realize how precious you are? Would you start from today to see yourself as a prince or princess? Can you face your detractors or problems knowing that you are of great value to God, that he will take care of you? This doesn't mean that your life is perfect, not at all; it means you are not alone, and God has got your back. That is our source of encouragement, hope, and joy. That's why St. Paul says in Philippians 4:4-6, "Rejoice always, I say it again rejoice." Is it possible to 'rejoice always' when we are sick or in pain, when a loved one dies, when we are financially broken or indebted, when experiencing a broken relationship, or when a family member is making wrong choices that will destroy their life, etc.? It isn't easy to rejoice in any of these situations. However, we are encouraged to rejoice because the Lord is near us, we are chosen and blessed by him, and we can bring everything to him in prayer, and he will give us peace. So, when life presents you with ten reasons to be worried, sad, and depressed, present it with 100 reasons to be happy and grateful because God is bigger than all your problems.

Trust in God, surrender to him, and permit him to walk with you along your life journey. He will help you to enjoy this life even in the midst your struggles, but above all, he will use your life to bless other people's lives, and in the end, he will lead you safely home to be with him for all eternity.

If only one person is encouraged after reading this book to see the experiences of life positively, use them to grow into becoming a better person, or use them as a stepping stone to achieve success in life and grow closer to Jesus, the purpose of this book will have been accomplished.

Suggested action: Take a banknote of any value and squeeze it hard until it wrinkles, then straighten it out again. Reflect on whether the wrinkles have diminished its value. Then, think about what could reduce your value as a child of God. Nothing – unless you permit it!

Prayer: Lord, thank you for the price you paid to redeem me. Please help me know that I am of great value and may nothing ever separate me from your love. Amen!

Appendix

Information about BAPOM Hospital and Family Care Program

Earlier in this book, I mentioned the birth of the Boniface and Paulina Okafor Memorial Hospital. For the interest of those who may like to know a little more about this project, I include brief information in the following pages.

Reason for choosing the name – BAPOM Hospital

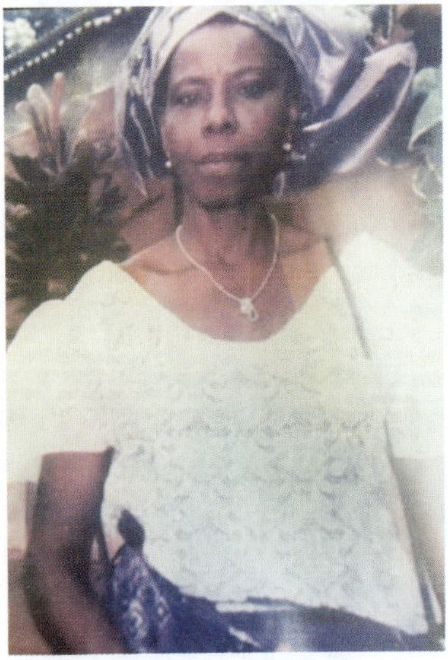

Mother: Paulina Okafor
Died April 1999

BAPOM Hospital stands for "Boniface and Paulina Okafor Memorial Hospital". Boniface and Paulina were my parents. They both had a great love for their community and were actively involved in many social activities that promoted human life and dignity. Even though they were not materially affluent, they generously shared what they had with those less fortunate than them. They reached out to the poor and the needy and positively touched many lives in the whole community. Paulina was diagnosed with diabetes when she was forty-six years old. Unfortunately, at that time, drugs (insulin) used for treating diabetes were very scarce and expensive in the Southeastern part of Nigeria. So, she had to travel to a hospital in the northern part of Nigeria, where the Nigerian government subsidized the drugs. The journey via train lasted for two or three days, and she had to go for routine checks every three to six months, depending on her sugar level. I give thanks to relatives living in the North who provided her with room and board, transportation, and basic needs. Later, she developed high blood pressure leading to complications, and eventually, she died at the age of sixty-six years.

Father: Mazi Boniface Madu Okafor – Died December 2006

In 2006, Boniface was diagnosed with cancer, which was very painful and expensive to treat. He died the same year. Their family and friends were there for them in their sickness, suffering, and pain. They appreciated the love, care, and support they received. In their last counsels, they encouraged all their children to love one another, to live in peace and unity, to avoid being attached to material things, and to continue to help the less privileged brothers and sisters in our society.

To honour them and continue their legacy of generous service to the community and care for the needy, when we started this project in 2016, we decided to name the hospital after them. Right now, their old

House currently used for the Clinic

house is being used as a temporary clinic, but it is our ardent desire to build a permanent hospital at another site.

Success Stories

Since the hospital opened in January 2017, it has offered free medical outreach four times. Over 1,200 patients received a free doctor's consultation and drugs and also a free consultation with an optometrist. Over 400 patients received free reading glasses.

Because of the clinic, many lives have been saved. We have received many testimonies and positive feedback from the patients and the medical doctor in charge of the clinic. For example, on February 15, 2017, the doctor wrote:

"Hello, Father. The work here is tedious, but I want to commend you and your team for helping your people. From what I saw recently, you may not know the number of people whose lives will be extended because of your generosity. Many of the men and women in your community are walking corpses. Sorry to use this word, but that's the truth. Some have elevated blood pressure and extremely high sugar levels. So incredible! I will try my best to bring them under control; many are already under control." (Dr. Anthony)

In August 2017, the doctor wrote:

"Hello, Father. I know that you have very good thoughts for your people, and I want to inform you that a

lot of them have benefitted from our clinic. A lot of them who would have died long ago are strong and are doing great now. We have reduced infant and maternal morbidity and mortality here and beyond this community. Many near-death sick patients are living healthier lives today. So, your effort is helping a lot of people. Many patients shower blessings on you and the benefactors before they leave the clinic. An indigent patient who I treated today said a short prayer for you. It's a pleasure to have this experience, and I think we are fulfilling God's will. Thanks a lot for this wonderful opportunity." (Dr. Anthony)

Also, in August 2017, the doctor reported:

"A man was bitten by a snake at midnight when he went out to urinate. He would have died before the day broke but, providentially, I was at the clinic that night, and I helped to save his life."

Help to families

Currently, through this program, forty-four children from low-income families receive scholarships to primary school, high school, and university. Eighteen low-income families are being provided with basic needs like food, medication, and housing. They are also helped with setting up small-scale businesses for economic self-reliance. The Clinic and Family Care Program beneficiaries send their gratitude and appreciation to all by gathering at the clinic every Wednesday to offer prayers for all the benefactors. These are indeed instruments of God's love and mercy. They positively impact people's lives and make a difference with their donations.

Some beneficiaries' testimonies

"I am Mr. Anthony Eze. I testify about what this hospital did for me regarding my healing from a peptic ulcer, severe chest pain, and heartburn. Within three days of my visit to Boniface & Paulina Okafor Memorial Hospital, through the treatment given by the doctor and the nurses, to the glory of God, I was healed of my illness which had troubled me for many years. The most wonderful thing was that the hospital bill was very low compared to what I spent at other hospitals. I am grateful to the management of this wonderful hospital under the directorship of Fr. Toochukwu and his Canadian Team. My prayer is that God may bless you and all the benefactors whom God has used to heal me."

"I am Mercy Onu. I testify to the goodness of God upon my life through Boniface & Paulina Okafor Memorial Hospital. Since I started visiting this hospital for treatment, I have always experienced quick recovery from all forms of ailments that have affected me. This clinic/hospital has been a Godsend to all my family members. Even my married daughter who lives outside our town always comes here with her own family. I appreciate Rev. Fr. Toochukwu and his team in Canada, who allowed God to use them to meet my health needs and that of our entire community. May God bless you all in Jesus' name, amen. I also thank the nurses and the doctor of this hospital for their care and dedication."

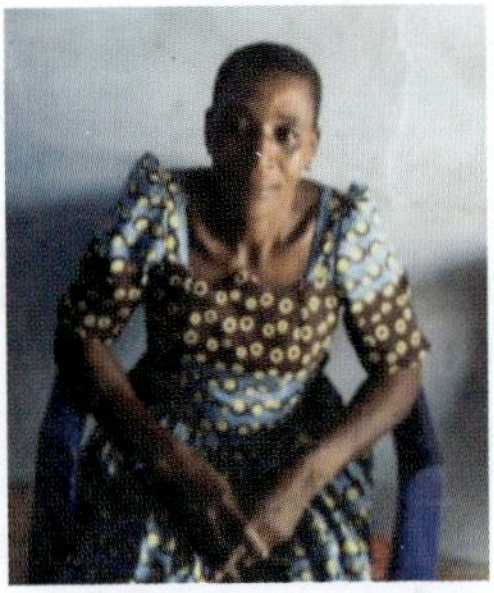

"My name is Elizabeth Igwe. I am happy to testify to what God did for me through the intervention of Boniface & Paulina Okafor Memorial Hospital. I have been going to different hospitals to find out my problem, but all to no avail. At B&P Hospital, it was discovered I had a lump in my breast. Through the help of the doctor and nurses at the hospital, I was cured. So, my appreciation goes to the management, Fr. Toochukwu Okafor, and our benefactors in Canada. My gratitude and praises go to the Almighty God for His divine healing in Jesus' name, amen."

With these reports, we can say that the organization's objectives and those of the medical clinic/hospital are being met. This would not have been possible without the help of the organizing team and the benefactors who supported this project with their time and monthly donations. We remain ever grateful to you all.

Many more families still need help, and the clinic still needs to be sustained to continue this noble mission. Presently, there are eight people on staff at the clinic. We raise funds in Canada and from anyone who wants to help to pay the team to make sure healthcare is affordable for the people. The clinic needs a laboratory, other hospital equipment, and a permanent house. Thanks to God and our benefactors, we have acquired fourteen plots of land where we could build the hospital.

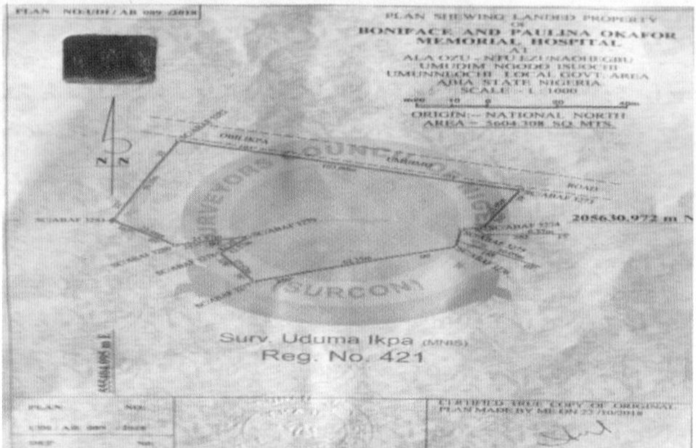

Future location of the BAPOM Hospital

We appreciate the generous support of all people of goodwill and pray that God may bless and reward them abundantly. Any help we receive will be deeply appreciated as it will enable us to help more people in need.

Free medical outreach, 2019 – over 300 people attended. Lorraine Coulombe traveled to Nigeria with me.

Elaine Young with a sponsored baby in Nigeria

Lorraine Coulombe with Beneficiaries when she visited the Clinic in Nigeria

Some Benefactors with Sr. Dr. Joannes when she visited Nova Scotia

Some sponsored children

If you wish to support this project, please contact:

bapomhospitalandfamilycare@gmail.com or

wearechosen2022@yahoo.com

Scripture quotations

The Catholic Youth Bible, NRSV Catholic Edition. Canada: Saint Mary's Press, 2011 (ISBN 9781599821351)

The New Community Bible, NCB Catholic Edition. Australia: St. Paul's Publications, 2012 (ISBN 9781921963148)

Good News Bible online version (https://www.biblestudytools.com/gnt/)